Where on Earth?
Understanding Latitude and Longitude

Robert A. Rutherfurd

J. Weston Walch, Publisher
Portland, Maine

1   2   3   4   5   6   7   8   9   10

ISBN 0-8251-1512-4

Copyright © 1989

J. Weston Walch, Publisher

P.O. Box 658 • Portland, Maine 04104-0658

Printed in the United States of America

Dedicated to

every geography teacher who has heard a
student say, "Those lines can't measure
east or west! They go north and south!"

CONTENTS

INTRODUCTION

Where on Earth? will be useful for either supplemental or basal work in most geography classes. Its materials are designed to help students:

- Read and follow directions carefully

- Produce neat and accurate work

- Understand latitude and longitude

- Use latitude and longitude to locate places on a map

- Use reference material to prepare projects and reports

- Gain knowledge of places and people around the world

Pages followed by *S* are meant for individual student use and should be reproduced in the appropriate number of copies. Pages followed by *T* have teaching suggestions and answer keys; generally they will not need to be copied. In some cases, though, copies of all or part of a *T* page may be helpful, particularly as a transparency for an overhead projector. Enlarging some diagrams before making transparencies, if a suitable copier is available, will enhance their usefulness.

The different materials in *Where on Earth?* are described below. They are intended to build skills in a definite sequence and should be used in the order presented in the book. *It is important that students have these Lessons (with vocabulary work), Activities (with worksheets), and Readings to study for the test. To ensure this, require that pupils keep completed assignments in folders or notebooks, preferably in the classroom.*

1. LESSONS The seven Lessons have material to be read, diagrams to be studied, and vocabulary to be defined. They make up the basic text of *Where on Earth?* and are suitable for either oral or silent work. Students will need access to dictionaries for the vocabulary work.

2. ACTIVITIES The sixteen Activities involve students in the use of grids and maps to develop an understanding of latitude and longitude. The work progresses from simple grids to world maps. These Activities stress accuracy and neatness; they reward the pupils with valuable learning tools they have helped create. Some of the advanced Activities introduce writing sentences to describe the relative location of places.

3. WORKSHEETS Ten Worksheets of grids or maps are provided to support work involved in the more advanced Activities. Students are usually asked to complete certain features of the Worksheets before using them; this develops skills and reinforces concepts.

4. READINGS Three Readings are provided to help clarify problems in using grids and to help students prepare for the Test. Since these Readings are designed for oral use and discussion, they have no written assignments.

5. RESEARCH The three sections on Research provide many ideas for reports and projects as well as suggestions for carrying them out and presenting them.

6. TEST   The Test involves using latitude and longitude to locate places on a map and to review skills, definitions, and concepts covered in *Where on Earth?* "Reading 3: Preparing for a Test" helps students get ready for the test. *Have students keep all completed assignments in folders or notebooks, preferably in the classroom, to study for this test.*

Understanding latitude and longitude is not always easy. It is hoped that *Where on Earth?* will help students grasp this important geography skill. Beyond that, this book's goal is also to help students work independently, create imaginatively, and communicate effectively. Most importantly, if *Where on Earth?* can stimulate an understanding of and an appreciation for the numerous and imaginative ways humans locate themselves on Planet Earth and make it their home, it will have done something of value.

Lesson 1: The Lines on a Map

A plane heads for a tiny island in the huge Pacific Ocean. Two nations prepare for war because of a dispute over a boundary line. A buyer refuses to purchase a parcel of land until a surveyor's stakes show him the exact property lines. You easily find a relative's rural home because of the orderly pattern of country roads crossing at right angles and at regular intervals.

What tool enables us to find that island or to place a boundary line between nations? What system establishes the lines between pieces of land or crosses our countryside with an orderly pattern of roads? The answer is *lines*—lines placed on a map in a definite pattern called a **grid**.

A grid is a set of evenly spaced horizontal (left-right) and vertical (up-down) lines that cross at right angles and form a pattern on which points can be precisely located. Window screens, checkerboards, and graph paper are common items that are forms of grids. Can you name others?

Using grids to locate places on the earth and to construct accurate maps was an inspiration that came to explorers and mapmakers centuries ago. It has proven to be a most useful idea and continues to serve humans well in a variety of ways. Activity B, which you will do soon, will illustrate how a simple grid works.

Definitions   Use a dictionary to find the meanings of the eight words below as they apply to maps or lines. Do these activities as directed by your teacher:

(a) On a separate sheet of paper, write a complete, accurate definition of each word.

(b) Use each word correctly in a good sentence.

(c) Be prepared to report orally on the pronunciation, meaning, and use of the words.

1. cartography	5. intersect
2. coordinate (n.)	6. parallel (adj.)
3. grid	7. right angle
4. horizontal	8. vertical

NOTE: KEEP THIS *LESSON* AND ITS *DEFINITIONS* WORK AND ALL FUTURE ONES FOR REVIEW PURPOSES.

Lesson 1:   Notes and Answers

"The Lines on a Map" may be read silently or orally. A classroom discussion using wall map, globe, and chalkboard will help students understand concepts. This can be done in conjunction with oral Definitions work. Point out to students that since map grids represent the surface of a spherical earth, they are not always perfect grids. For example, the lines on maps are not always parallel and do not always intersect at right angles. Other common items using grids are: tiled floors, paned windows, and pizza parlor tablecloths.

Definitions   Be sure students know which activities are to be done. Remind them to note part-of-speech abbreviations and to keep definitions relevant. Encourage students to make their definitions as complete and accurate as possible.

1. cartography
   - (a) the science of mapmaking; the study of maps
   - (b) *Cartography* today produces many different kinds of world maps.

2. coordinate (n.)
   - (a) a number used to locate a point or line
   - (b) The pilot checked the *coordinates* of the airport before the flight.

3. grid
   - (a) a pattern of vertical and horizontal lines used to locate points
   - (b) Use the *grid* on this map to determine the coordinates of the state capital.

4. horizontal
   - (a) running left and right, parallel with the horizon
   - (b) The surveyor established a *horizontal* line for the foundation.

5. intersect
   - (a) to meet and cross one another
   - (b) This street does not *intersect* the highway.

6. parallel (adj.)
   - (a) running the same direction and always the same distance apart
   - (b) The rails of the railroad track are *parallel*.

7. right angle
   - (a) an angle formed by perpendicular lines; a 90-degree angle
   - (b) Many streets cross at *right angles*.

8. vertical
   - (a) running straight up and down, perpendicular to the horizon
   - (b) The wallpaper has a pattern of *vertical* lines.

HAVE STUDENTS KEEP THIS *LESSON* AND ITS *DEFINITIONS* WORK AND ALL FUTURE ONES FOR REVIEW PURPOSES.

Activity A: Neat Labels

As you do the activities about locations on the earth, you will be placing many names on grids and maps. Printing these names clearly will be very important. Pay close attention to the specific directions given by your teacher; then do the work below.

A. *Print* each name neatly in the space provided.

1. Rocky Mountains   Rocky   _____

2. Lake Michigan   _____   _____

3. Salt Lake City   _____   _____   _____

4. Columbia River   _____   _____

5. Gulf of Mexico   _____   _____   _____

B. *Print* each answer neatly in the space provided. Spell correctly and abbreviate only if necessary.

1. Your state   _____

2. Your city   _____

3. Your school   _____

4. A nearby street   _____

5. A nearby store   _____

Where on Earth? Understanding Latitude and Longitude

Activity A: Neat Labels *(continued)*

C. Assume space is limited and you must correctly abbreviate the one most appropriate word in each name that follows. *Print* the name neatly in the space provided. Use a dictionary if necessary. Where there is no line, take care to keep printing straight.

1. Mount Kilimanjaro   Mt. _____

2. Strait of Gibraltar   _____ ____ _____

3. Mississippi River   _____ _____

4. Aleutian Islands

5. Lake Winnipegosis

D. Use an almanac, atlas, or other reference material to find each answer. Then *print* the full name neatly in the space provided. Abbreviate only if necessary. Where there is no line, take care to keep printing straight.

1. World's longest river   _____ River _____

2. World's largest ocean   _____ _____

3. World's highest mountain

4. Africa's largest lake

5. World's largest island

NOTE: KEEP THIS *ACTIVITY* AND ALL FUTURE ONES FOR REVIEW PURPOSES.

Activity A: Notes and Answers

"Neat Labels" should be presented as an important first activity because it gives students a chance to practice neat, clear work. It will also condition them to read and follow directions carefully.

Before students work, stress the guidelines they should use when labeling grids and maps. A suggested list is given below. Put the guidelines on the side of the chalkboard or on a poster where they can be seen and reviewed often.

1. Read and follow all directions carefully.

2. Use printing to label grids and maps.

3. Work first in pencil. When work is correct, go over it with pen or fine-point marker.

4. Use only dark blue or black for lettering.

5. Use a straightedge or penciled lines to keep lettering straight.

6. Erase remains of penciled lettering and lines, being careful not to smear work.

7. Allow plenty of time for work so you don't have to rush.

Answers   Consider both neatness and accuracy when papers are evaluated. It is suggested that teachers encourage students to print in lowercase except for capitalization. This would be a good time to discuss how printing in all capitals may be used for stress or clarity, as is the case on maps and reproducible materials like the ones in this book.

A.
1. Rocky Mountains
2. Lake Michigan
3. Salt Lake City
4. Columbia River
5. Gulf of Mexico

B.
1.
2.
3. Answers vary. Stress correct spelling and, if
4. used, abbreviations.
5.

C.
1. Mt. Kilimanjaro
2. Str. of Gibraltar
3. Mississippi R.
4. Aleutian Is.
5. L. Winnepegosis

D.
1. Nile River
2. Pacific Ocean
3. Mount Everest
4. Lake Tanganyika
5. Greenland

HAVE STUDENTS KEEP THIS *ACTIVITY* AND ALL FUTURE ONES FOR REVIEW PURPOSES.

Activity B: A Simple Grid

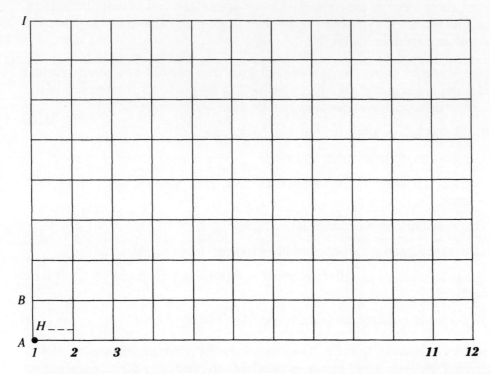

Directions: Before doing the work below, complete the identification of the lines in this grid by putting on the missing letters and numbers. The letters and numbers identify the *lines* and should be placed clearly right by the lines they identify.

A.   Print the letter of the correct answer in the blank in front of the number.

_____ 1. The numbers on the grid identify the (a) horizontal (b) vertical lines.

_____ 2. The letters on the grid identify the (a) horizontal (b) vertical lines.

_____ 3. Label the dot on the grid "Home." Home is located at (a) B1 (b) A1 (c) A3.

B.   Use the letters and numbers to mark these places on the grid with dots like the one for "Home." Label each dot with the proper name.

<u>D12</u> 1. School	<u>E5</u> 5. Church	<u>F9</u> 9. Grocery Store
<u>C11</u> 2. Pet Shop	<u>A8</u> 6. Drugstore	<u>H10</u> 10. Post Office
<u>B4</u> 3. Alice's	<u>D1</u> 7. Frank's	<u>G7</u> 11. Aunt Clara's
<u>H2</u> 4. Bus Stop	<u>C6</u> 8. Movie	<u>I3</u> 12. Mrs. Price's

Where on Earth? Understanding Latitude and Longitude

Activity B: Notes and Key

Remind students to work neatly and follow directions carefully. The labeling of the grid lines, which stresses that the *lines* do the measuring, is important. The activity then shows how the crossing of two lines locates an exact point. Discuss this concept of coordinates and illustrate it on the chalkboard.

Key and Answers   Stress neatness and clarity in evaluating work. Use an overhead transparency of the key to ensure that students understand this grid. Use vocabulary words from Lesson 1 in discussing it.

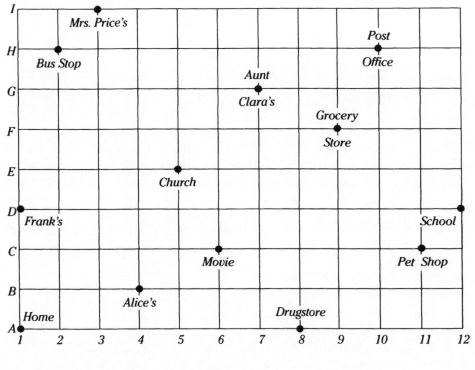

A. 1. <u>b</u>   2. <u>a</u>   3. <u>b</u>

Discussion Questions   Use these questions orally to reinforce concepts covered in earlier work:

1. Does a mountain or other physical feature serve as the starting point for local surveying?

2. Are local streets oriented in the cardinal compass directions? Could some addresses be confused without compass directions? Do some streets bear names related to their locations—Main, Meridian, First, A, etc?

3. Are there local boundaries—county, state, national—based on map grid lines? What natural features are used for boundary lines when grid lines are not?

Where on Earth? Understanding Latitude and Longitude

Reading 1:   How Grid Lines Measure

There is an interesting and important point to notice when using a grid—or any scale—to measure a distance. THE LINES THAT ACTUALLY MEASURE A DISTANCE DO NOT RUN THE SAME DIRECTION AS THAT DISTANCE; INSTEAD, THEY CUT ACROSS IT AT RIGHT ANGLES. Notice how this idea applies to a ruler:

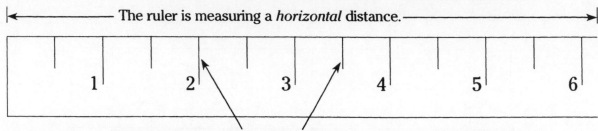

|← The ruler is measuring a *horizontal* distance. →|

The measuring marks are *vertical*.

This ruler measures a horizontal distance from left to right. However, without the vertical measuring marks it would be useless. It is these vertical marks, running at right angles to the distance being measured, that do the actual measuring. Notice how this same idea applies to a grid.

This grid illustrates how the lines that do the measuring cut across the distance being measured. Even though the numbers measure a horizontal (east-west) distance, they identify vertical (north-south) lines to do so. In a similar way the letters, which form a vertical scale to measure north-south distance, identify horizontal lines.

Work with this concept until you understand it well. It will be a great help in using grids to locate places on maps.

NOTE: KEEP THIS *READING* AND ALL FUTURE ONES FOR REVIEW PURPOSES.

The *horizontal* lines, labeled by the letters, measure the *vertical* (north-south) distance.

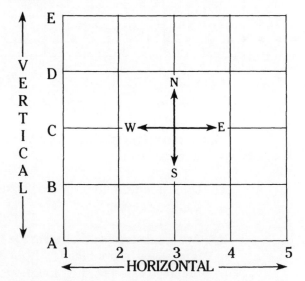

The *vertical* lines, labeled by the numbers, measure the *horizontal* (east-west) distance.

Reading 1:   Discussion Notes

"How Grid Lines Measure" is intended for classroom reading and discussion. After reading the selection silently, students should read it aloud and discuss any problems with understanding. Talk about the two illustrations and use this diagram on the chalkboard:

Ask this question about the drawing: Within this square, in which direction may I measure distances, A or B? As the correct answer, B, develops, point out that the box contains *vertical* lines, which allow only *horizontal* distances to be determined. Even though students see a preponderance of vertical lines, at present there is no way to measure a vertical distance in the box. Relate this to a wall map of the world by showing how the vertical lines (meridians) measure east-west (horizontal) distances.

Vocabulary Also use the wall map to show how the vocabulary related to direction is changing. *Up-down* became *vertical*, for which *north-south* is now being used. *Left-right* went to *horizontal* and is now *east-west*. As you show students how the cardinal compass directions run on a standard world map—north to the top, east to the right, etc.—discuss where these four directions lie in relation to your own classroom. Inform the students that *most* maps, *but not all*, have north at the top. Also caution them that *up* or *down* on maps has nothing to do with the direction of water flow, which is caused by elevation. Use the Nile River to illustrate this.

Printing   Have students practice printing the following words neatly from dictation. They will be using them soon in activities on grids and maps. Point out locations on a wall map and give spelling help as needed.

Jakarta	New Delhi	Tokyo
Lima	Nome	Wellington
South Georgia Island	Pretoria	
Mexico City	Seattle	

HAVE STUDENTS KEEP THIS *READING* AND ALL FUTURE ONES FOR REVIEW PURPOSES.

Activity C: Line Battleship I

Complete the scales by writing the correct missing letters and numbers by the lines.

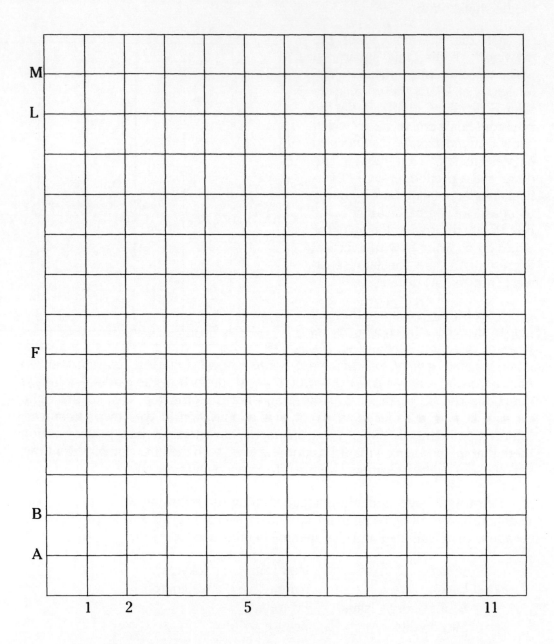

Activity C: Notes

Some students may be familiar with the game "Battleship."* "Line Battleship" is similar, with the exception that the intersections of the lines, rather than the squares of the grids, are location points. This makes playing "Line Battleship" similar to using latitude and longitude on a map.

Students play "Line Battleship" in pairs, with one of the two familiar with the game, if possible. Go over the following rules first, listing some on the chalkboard if needed. Supervise students as they play, making sure they use the lines and coordinates of the grid correctly. Collect and grade papers on neatness and completeness.

1. Complete the scales by identifying the lines with the necessary letters and numbers.
2. Locate four ships anywhere on your grid, except the margins, with the following symbols. Don't let your opponent see the locations of your ships.

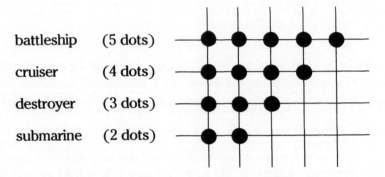

3. Take turns firing 3 shots at the opponent's ships by giving the coordinates of the intersecting lines—B5, E7, etc. Keep track of your shots with circles.

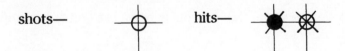

4. Keep track of hits on both sides' ships by placing an X over the dot or circle.
5. You must tell the opponent of any hit or sinking in your fleet and identify the type of ship hit or sunk.
6. The first person to sink all the opponent's ships is the winner.

There are many variations in the number and size of ships and the system of shooting that imaginative students can incorporate into this game. The important thing is that they practice using the coordinates on a grid to establish exact locations.

---

* Milton Bradley puts out a durable plastic commercial version of this game.

Activity D: An Advanced Grid

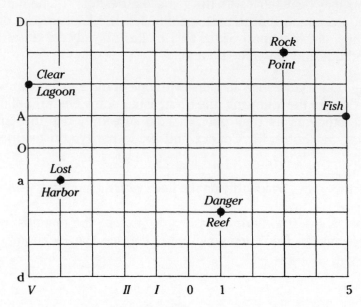

Directions   Before doing the work below, complete the identification of the lines on this grid by putting on the missing letters and numbers. Be sure to make them *capital* or *small*, *roman* or *arabic*, just as they have been started.

A. Print the letter of the correct answer in the blank in front of the number.

_____ 1. Place a large dot at 00, which is the point at which the two zero lines cross. Label it "Home." Home's location is at the (a) center (b) corner of the grid.

_____ 2. The (a) horizontal (b) vertical lines on the grid are identified by the letters.

_____ 3. The (a) horizontal (b) vertical lines on the grid are identified by the numbers.

B. Referring to the grid, put the locating letter, then number, *in that order*, in the blanks in front of the first four places below. Use the letters and numbers of the last eight places to find their locations on the grid. Mark them with large dots and label them with their names.

C	1. Rock Point	A5	5. Fish Inlet	dIII	9. Pirate Beach
IV	2. Lost Harbor	DII	6. Safety Bay	CO	10. Poison Spring
___	3. Clear Lagoon	OI	7. Sand Island	a4	11. Crystal River
___	4. Danger Reef	A3	8. Stormy Gulf	c4	12. Cemetery Cove

Where on Earth? Understanding Latitude and Longitude

Activity D: Notes and Key

Remind students to read directions carefully before doing any work. Tell them that the scale on this advanced grid is different from the one on the simple grid and that they should work carefully as they label the lines. Through either class discussion, using the chalkboard, or individual help, make sure the students know how to use this new grid.

Key and Answers Emphasize the importance of neatness in completed work. This can be done by having students exchange papers and evaluate the work of others. Use an overhead transparency of this key in a class discussion and encourage students to illustrate how the grid works. At this time the progression of left-right to horizontal to east-west and up-down to vertical to north-south can be pointed out. And if it seems appropriate, the awkwardness of using two kinds of letters and numbers in this grid might be brought out. Ask students to suggest possible alternatives and help them see that the use of a number and a compass direction will be the ultimate answer.

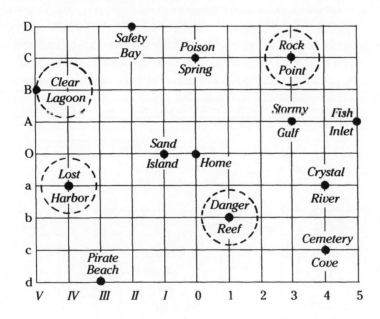

A. 1. <u>a</u>   2. <u>a</u>   3. <u>b</u>

B.   <u>C3</u>   1. Rock Point   <u>BV</u>   3. Clear Lagoon

          <u>aIV</u>   2. Lost Harbor   <u>b1</u>   4. Danger Reef

© 1989 J. Weston Walch, Publisher   *Where on Earth? Understanding Latitude and Longitude*

Reading 2:   How Map Grids Are Labeled

Each grid line on a map must have its unique label so it will not be confused with any other grid line. But a grid that uses two different kinds of letters and two different kinds of numbers, as in Activity D, is very awkward. It would be a poor system to use in locating places on the earth.

What system do we use—letters, numbers, symbols? Numbers have proven to be the best labels to use for grid lines on a map. There are many more of them than the twenty-six letters of the alphabet, and they can be divided easily into fractional parts for fixing precise locations. Furthermore, the Roman numerals are not used, just the Arabic ones.

But now we have to ask, "With only numbers being used to label lines on a map grid, how can one tell if a measurement is to the north, south, east, or west?" That question just about answers itself. To the number that tells how far from the starting line one goes is added one word—*north, south, east,* or *west.*

The illustrations below show how these map grid scales work. On a real map the numbers, of course, go much higher than five. Notice that each number does not have the compass direction written with it. The compass directions will usually be indicated somewhere on the map, perhaps only with initials. Just about all maps have north at the top, east to the right, south to the bottom, and west to the left. Learn these directions as you study these scales. Notice also how the lines that do the measuring run at right angles to the distance being measured.

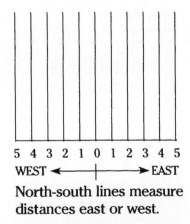

5 4 3 2 1 0 1 2 3 4 5
WEST ◄——————|——————► EAST

North-south lines measure distances east or west.

East-west lines measure distances north or south.

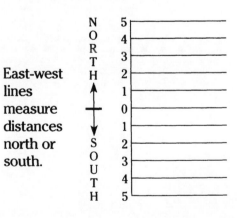

The point to remember is this: EVERY LABEL FOR A LINE ON A MAP GRID HAS TWO PARTS—A *NUMBER* THAT MEASURES HOW FAR FROM THE STARTING POINT (ZERO) THE LINE IS AND A *COMPASS DIRECTION* THAT TELLS IN WHICH DIRECTION FROM THE STARTING POINT THE MEASUREMENT GOES.

Where on Earth? Understanding Latitude and Longitude

Reading 2:   Discussion Notes

Use "How Map Grids Are Labeled" for class reading followed by discussion. It may be read silently and/or aloud. After the reading provide clarification for any problems students had with understanding.

Discussion Questions   Use these questions for class discussion:

1. Why is the grid labeling system in Activity D, "An Advanced Grid," awkward to use? (The numerals have to be designated Roman or Arabic, and the letters must be described as small or capital.)

2. What is an advantage of using only Arabic numerals to identify map grid lines? (They are widely understood. They form many numbers, which may be divided into fractional parts.)

3. What question arises when only numbers are used to label map grid lines? (In what direction is the measurement going?)

4. How is the question raised above answered? (*North, south, east,* or *west* is always added to the number.)

5. Which way do the compass directions run on almost all maps? (North is to the top, east to the right, south to the bottom, and west to the left.)

Visual   Use this diagram on the chalkboard or as an overhead transparency. It is a grid that combines the two scales from the reading's illustrations. Use the ● and the **X** to explain how the grid works. Drill students by putting more dots on the grid and asking for coordinates or by giving coordinates and asking students to point out the locations.

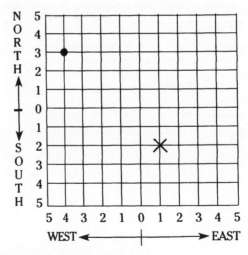

The ● is at 3 north, 4 west.
The **X** is at 2 south, 1 east.

Notes:

Where on Earth? Understanding Latitude and Longitude

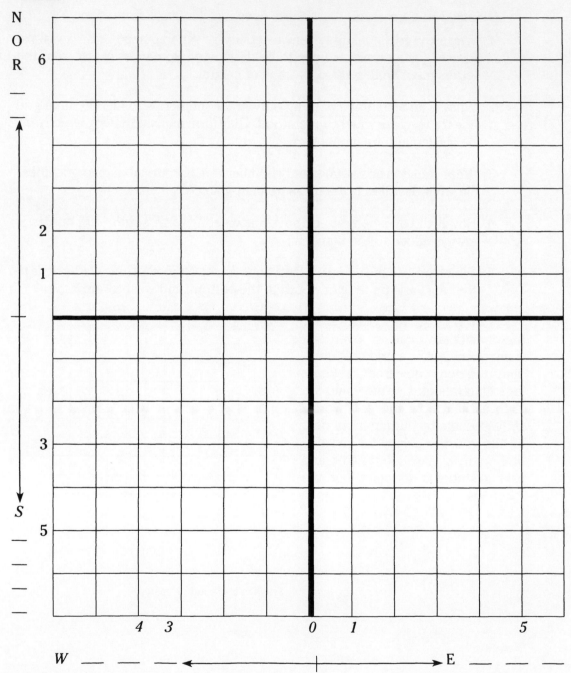

Name: _____ Date: _____ *16S*

Activity E: Line Battleship II

Complete the scales by writing the correct missing numbers by the lines. Complete the compass directions by printing the correct missing letters in the blanks.

Where on Earth? Understanding Latitude and Longitude

Activity E: Notes

"Line Battleship II" is the same game as "Line Battleship I" with the exception of the grid. The grid in "Line Battleship II" uses numbers and cardinal compass directions as the coordinates for locations. Refer to the notes on Activity C, page 11, to refresh students on the rules.

Caution students to work carefully to complete the scales identifying the lines. Both boldfaced center lines are zero lines. Margin lines are not labeled; this cuts down the number of possible locations to speed up the game. Tell students to say the number first, then the direction, when giving coordinates: 4 East, 5 South.

Enrichment   If it seems appropriate, briefly discuss similarities between the grid for this game and the grids on world maps. The boldfaced horizontal line at 0 resembles the *equator*, the starting point for measuring north-south distances on the earth. The boldfaced vertical line at 0 is like the *prime meridian (Greenwich Meridian)*, the starting point for measuring east-west distances on the earth. Use a wall map of the world to point out these two lines.

Students may be asking what the scale numbers stand for. Point out that the numbers on the scales are not simply numerical symbols used to identify lines. The numbers on map grids do represent units of measurement, but not miles or kilometers. Since the earth is a sphere with a circular cross section, the units for measuring a circle, *degrees*, are used to locate and identify the lines on a map grid. It will be helpful, and relatively easy, for students, as they play "Line Battleship II," to say "degrees" after each number as they give coordinates.

Activity   Many maps make use of a locator grid in which the squares, rather than the intersecting lines, are labeled with numbers and/or letters. The indexes for such maps will give the coordinates for the square in which an item such as a city or street will be found. Often the location of the square must be estimated because the lines for these grids are usually not drawn on the map. Have students locate items on road, city, or other maps using this system. Discuss the advantages and disadvantages of both "square" and "intersecting line" grids and help students see that the intersecting lines are a much more precise system.

Notes:

Where on Earth? Understanding Latitude and Longitude

Lesson 2:   Map Grid Measurements

Now that only numbers are being used to identify the lines on our grids, we might ask, "On real map grids what do these numbers stand for?" They *do not* stand for commonly used measures of distance such as miles or kilometers. They *do* represent **degrees**, the units used to measure angles or parts of circles.

A degree may be thought of as a tiny piece of pie. 360 of these tiny pieces, or degrees, make a complete circle; 90 of them make a right angle. The symbol for degrees is a small circle placed above and after the number. For example, "60° N" means "60 degrees North." Because the earth is so large, there can be considerable distance in one degree. Therefore, each degree is divided into 60 **minutes**, and each minute is further divided into 60 **seconds**. This division of each degree into 3,600 parts permits great precision in determining locations on the earth.

Since the earth is a sphere, if it is cut in half directly through the center, the cross section will be a circle. In locating grid lines on the earth, we think of moving along the edge of these cross sections or circles. First we picture a line going from our starting point at 0° to the center of the earth. Then we go in a straight north, south, east, or west direction to the point we want to locate. We now imagine a second line running to the center of the earth to form an angle with the first line. The number of degrees in this angle, along with the compass direction traveled, is the label for the grid line at this new location.

How it works: Use this diagram to see how degrees are used to locate map grid lines. To determine 60° N we go north from 0° until angle *a*, a 60° angle, is formed. We place an east-west line, line *d*, at this point on the map grid. Any location along line *d* is 60 degrees north of the zero starting point.

Our intersecting north-south line, line *c*, is located by going east from 0° until angle *b*, a 45° angle, is formed. Any point along line *c* is located 45 degrees east of the zero starting point. The circled intersection of lines *c* and *d* is a precise location on the earth that cannot be confused with any other. It is 60° N, 45° E.

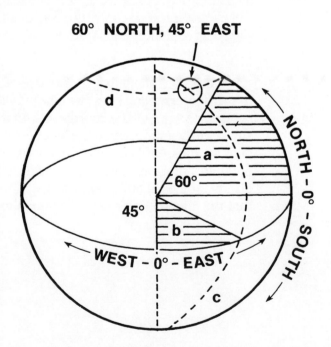

60° NORTH, 45° EAST

Lesson 2: Map Grid Measurements *(continued)*

Getting things right Because you have been using grids with straight lines, you may be bothered by the curving grid lines on the diagram. Remember that the diagram shows the earth as it really is—a sphere. Any lines on its curved surface must also curve. When we make a map of the world, we "peel off the skin," in a sense, and lay it flat. In doing so, we also straighten out the grid lines. However, many maps retain some degree of curve in the grid lines. Be on the lookout for these curving grid lines on the different maps you use.

Using degrees to locate lines on the earth's surface is using **angular distance**, which is very different from the normal idea of distance. Angular distance has to do with "Where?" rather than with "How far away?" At some places on the earth there are many miles between degrees, while at other locations the degrees are very close together. So degrees must be used carefully to tell how far from each other places are. On the other hand, degrees are the highly accurate measures that tell us exactly "where on earth" a place is.

Definitions Use a dictionary to find the meanings of the six words below as they apply to measuring in degrees. Do these activities as directed by your teacher:

(a) On a separate sheet of paper, write a complete, accurate definition of each word.

(b) Use each word correctly in a good sentence.

(c) Be prepared to report orally on the pronunciation, meaning, and use of the words.

1. angle (n.)   4. protractor
2. degree   5. second (n.)
3. minute (n.)   6. vertex

Lesson 2:   Notes and Answers

Students will need to read "Map Grid Measurements" and study its diagram carefully in order to understand the concepts presented. Oral reading and class discussion will be needed to assure understanding. It will help to supplement them with an overhead transparency of the diagram as well as a world wall map and a globe.

The way in which different school subjects are related can be pointed out easily as this subject is discussed, for this geography lesson deals with basic geometry concepts. Use this chance to tell students that success in one subject can help lead to success in another.

Definitions   Be sure students know which activities are to be done. Remind them to note part-of-speech abbreviations and to keep definitions relevant.

1. angle (n.)
   (a) the figure formed between two straight lines that meet
   (b) There is an *angle* at each corner of a triangle.

2. degree
   (a) the unit used in measuring angles
   (b) A right angle contains 90 *degrees.*

3. minute (n.)
   (a) 1/60 of a degree in an angle; symbol: '
   (b) A degree of an angle is divided into 60 *minutes.*

4. protractor
   (a) an instrument used to measure or draw angles
   (b) He used a *protractor* to make a diagram showing grid lines on the earth.

5. second (n.)
   (a) 1/3600 of a degree in an angle; symbol: "
   (b) An exact location may be given in degrees, minutes, and *seconds.*

6. vertex
   (a) the meeting point for the two sides of an angle
   (b) In the diagram the center of the earth was the *vertex* of several angles.

Notes:

Activity F: Latitude—North or South

In doing Activity F you will work on a separate paper handed out by your teacher. This Worksheet F has a grid on it similar to the grid of an actual world map. On this grid you will show the location north or south of ten real places on the earth. This measurement of a north or south location on the earth is called **latitude**. Lesson 3 on page 25 will discuss latitude in more detail.

A. Preparing the grid   Complete the worksheet grid by neatly and carefully finishing the required lettering or numbering of these items:

1. Title: LATITUDE

4. Scale labels: Degrees, North, South

2. 0° Line: EQUATOR

5. Scale numbers: 0 to 90

3. Directions: NORTH, SOUTH

B. Finding the locations   Use the scale and compass directions to find the location of the latitude of each of the ten places listed below. Use a straightedge to draw a dotted line at each latitude completely across the grid. Label each dotted line near the left margin with the name and latitude of the place it locates.

1. Jakarta (Indonesia) . . . 6° S

2. Lima (Peru) . . . 12° S

3. Mexico City (Mexico) . . . 19° N

4. New Delhi (India) . . . 29° N

5. Nome (Alaska) . . . 65° N

6. Pretoria (South Africa) . . . 26° S

7. Seattle (Washington) . . . 48° N

8. South Georgia Island (South Atlantic Ocean) . . . 54° S

9. Tokyo (Japan) . . . 36° N

10. Wellington (New Zealand) . . . 41° S

Note: Do not put the information in parentheses on your grid. It is given simply to help you know in a general way where each place is.

On this grid you do not show the exact location of each place, but you do show its location north or south of the equator. Adding a correctly placed vertical line will create an intersection showing exactly where on earth each place is. You will be doing that very soon in activities to come.

Name: _____   Date: _____   22S

Worksheet F: **Grid**

LATI _____

Degrees N

Degrees S

D — North

D — South

90 80   20 10 0   50 60   90

90   30   0 10   90

N O R _____

E Q U _____

S O _____

19° N

Jakarta 6° S

Lima

Activity F: Notes

Be sure that students receive both the instruction sheet and the worksheet for Activity F. Tell them that it will be very important to work carefully and neatly on the worksheet. Reviewing the guidelines for neat work on page 4T will not only give students helpful tips, but will also remind them of your expectations.

Encourage the careful reading and following of directions by refraining from giving students any but the most essential help. Most of them should be able to do this work completely on their own. A good technique is to have those who seem helplessly stumped get assistance from a student who was able to master the work without any help.

It is also recommended that second worksheets not be given to students who ruin the first one with careless mistakes. Instead, they can be told to use $\frac{1}{4}$-inch graph paper to make a new one. The worksheet has been constructed on graph paper with a $\frac{1}{4}$-inch grid. This permits students to construct a replacement quite easily and to remind themselves in the process of the value of doing neat, careful work.

Key   The key for Worksheet F on page 24T has a key along the margin to help in checking papers. Of course, the location of some lines may vary slightly on student work. Evaluate papers not only on completeness and accuracy, but on neatness, legibility, and use of a straightedge for good lines and a pen or a marker for sharp labels.

Visual   An overhead transparency of the key can help classes by illustrating the desired type of grid. Such points as accuracy, neatness, and clarity may be discussed. The projected grid can be compared to a world wall map—perhaps even projected right on or next to it. Imagining an east-west dotted line from the grid at its relative location on a world map should run the line through or near the place it locates. Students should be involved in this activity. The parenthetical location information on the instruction sheet should help them find the ten places on the map.

As these places are located and named, discuss what and where they are: capital cities, harbors, sites of past or current events, etc. In other words, use these discussions to make geography relevant and current.

Notes:

Activity F: Key

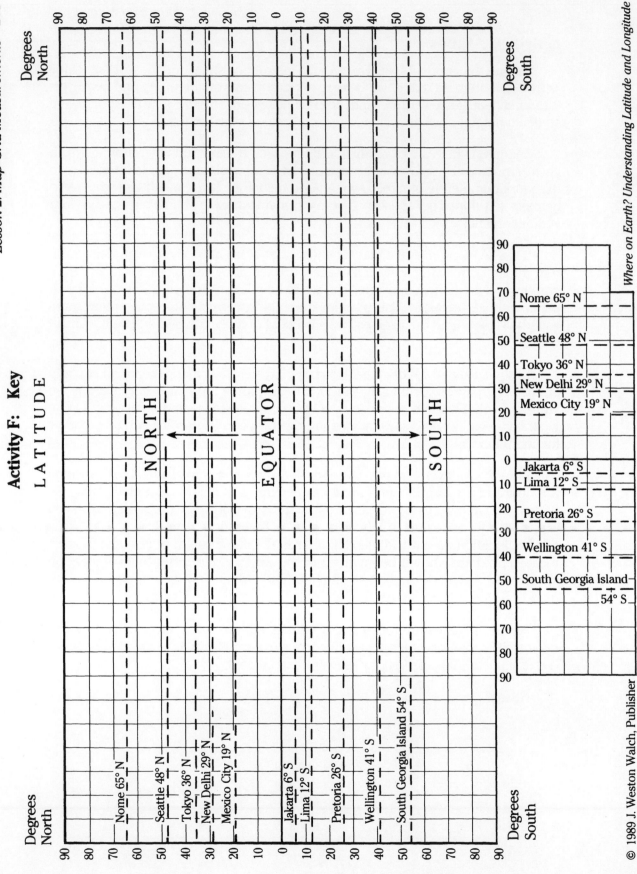

LATITUDE

Degrees North

Nome 65° N
Seattle 48° N
Tokyo 36° N
New Delhi 29° N
Mexico City 19° N

NORTH

EQUATOR

SOUTH

Jakarta 6° S
Lima 12° S
Pretoria 26° S
Wellington 41° S
South Georgia Island 54° S

Degrees South

Degrees North

Nome 65° N
Seattle 48° N
Tokyo 36° N
New Delhi 29° N
Mexico City 19° N

Jakarta 6° S
Lima 12° S
Pretoria 26° S
Wellington 41° S
South Georgia Island 54° S

Degrees South

Where on Earth? Understanding Latitude and Longitude

Lesson 3:   What Is Latitude?

In simple terms **latitude** is how far north or south from the equator a place is. Since many locations on the earth must be fixed very precisely, latitude has to be defined more completely.

To be more precise, **latitude is the angular distance due north or south from the equator of a location on the earth.**

This diagram of a polar cross section of the earth will help you understand how latitude works. First, **angular distance** means that latitude is measured in terms of an angle, so it is expressed in degrees. Lesson 2 explained this aspect of latitude quite thoroughly.

Second, **due north or south** means that the angle measuring latitude runs straight north or south. A good way to picture this is to think of the angle of any latitude as a wedge or piece of pie standing on edge on the equator. It stands at right angles to the equator, and its edge runs exactly in a north-south direction.

Finally, **from the equator** tells us that the equator is the starting point for measuring latitude. The equator, an imaginary east-west line, circles the center of the earth midway between the North Pole and the South Pole. Its location is 0° latitude. As locations are found further north or south, the angle between them and the equator increases and the number of degrees indicating their latitude gets larger.

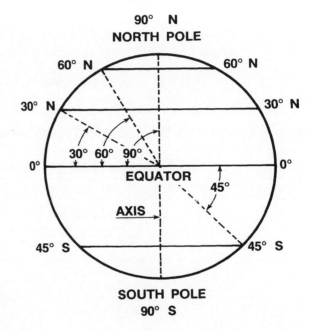

How high can a reading of latitude go? Since latitude concerns the angle from the equator to the poles, which is one quarter of a circle, latitude readings will always range from 0° at the equator to 90° at the poles. Of course, except for the equator, the designation *north* or *south* must always be given with the number of degrees of latitude.

Where on Earth? Understanding Latitude and Longitude

Lesson 3:   What Is Latitude? *(continued)*

A latitude measurement is marked on a world map in the form of an east-west line. (You already did this for ten places in Activity F.) A place on earth with that latitude will be located somewhere on that line. Because the lines that represent various latitudes all run in the same east-west direction and never cross, they are called **parallels**.

With measurements of latitude, people have been able to explore, map, and use the earth with great accuracy. This is because latitude is an extremely precise tool for telling "where on earth" things are. Its discovery and use certainly give testimony to the ingenuity of humans and have permitted them to make great advances.

Definitions   Use a dictionary to find the meanings of the six words below as they apply to latitude and directions. Do these activities as directed by your teacher:

(a) On a separate sheet of paper, write a complete, accurate definition of each word.

(b) Use each word correctly in a good sentence.

(c) Be prepared to report orally on the pronunciation, meaning, and use of the words.

1. cardinal points
2. equator
3. latitude
4. parallel (n.)
5. pole (n.)
6. polestar

Where on Earth? Understanding Latitude and Longitude

Lesson 3:   Notes and Answers

Students will comprehend "What Is Latitude?" best if it is read orally and discussed thoroughly. Refer to the diagram frequently, using an overhead transparency or a chalkboard copy. Use a world wall map and a globe to illustrate concepts. Involve students by having them explain certain material to the rest of the class. Encourage the use of the Definitions words from this lesson and the two earlier ones.

Definitions   Be sure students know which activities are to be done. Remind them to note part-of-speech abbreviations and to keep definitions relevant. Always use plenty of oral work with the Definitions material to ensure that students pronounce and use the words correctly.

1. cardinal points
    (a) the primary directions on a compass: north, south, east, and west
    (b) The *cardinal points* are clearly marked on this compass.

2. equator
    (a) an imaginary line circling the earth midway between the North Pole and the South Pole
    (b) The *equator* does not pass through the United States.

3. latitude
    (a) the angular distance due north or south from the equator of a location on the earth
    (b) Each day the navigator determined the ship's *latitude.*

4. parallel (n.)
    (a) an imaginary east-west line circling the earth parallel to the equator, used to measure latitude
    (b) The two countries decided to use a *parallel* of latitude as a common boundary line.

5. pole (n.)
    (a) the point at the end of the earth's axis; the North Pole or the South Pole
    (b) Roald Amundsen was the first explorer to reach the South *Pole.*

6. polestar
    (a) Polaris; the North Star; an aid in determining latitude because it is over the North Pole
    (b) The *polestar* helped many early sailors determine their approximate latitude.

Notes:

Research 1:   Latitude Projects

Do any of these projects as your teacher may direct for regular class assignments or extra-credit work. Do your best to produce neat, well-organized material.

1. Polar Map   North is not always at the top of all maps. Study a polar map of either the North Pole or the South Pole. Answer the questions below as you write a report describing what you observe about the grid lines and the compass directions. Attach a colored, labeled copy of the map to your report.

(a) Which polar map are you describing? What compass direction is toward its center? Toward its edges?

(b) What compass directions are represented by straight lines? By circles or curved lines?

(c) At the pole, what happens to the grid lines? What happens to each of the four compass directions?

(d) Which compass direction is clockwise? Counterclockwise? What advantages, if any, does this kind of map have?

2. Navigation tools   Prepare a report and illustration(s) for one or more of these topics:

(a) astrolabe   (d) gyrocompass
(b) compass   (e) quadrant
(c) cross-staff   (f) sextant

3. Latitude distances   Compute the approximate distance on the earth for each of the following measurements of latitude. Be sure to use the polar circumference of the earth. Round answers to one or two decimal places.

(a) There are _____ miles in one degree of latitude. (circumference of the earth _____ / _____ number of degrees in a complete circle)

(b) There are _____ miles in one minute of latitude. (answer to Part a _____ / _____ number of minutes in one degree)

(c) There is _____ (decimal fraction) of a mile in one second of latitude. (answer to Part b _____ / _____ number of seconds in one minute)

(d) There are _____ feet in one second of latitude. (answer to Part c _____ × _____ number of feet in one mile)

Where on Earth? Understanding Latitude and Longitude

Research 1:   Latitude Projects *(continued)*

4. Special parallels   Define these four terms and give their latitude readings:

   (a) Arctic Circle
   (b) Antarctic Circle
   (c) Tropic of Cancer
   (d) Tropic of Capricorn

   Locate these parallels on a diagram of a polar cross section of the earth. Also indicate the earth's axis, poles, and equator.

   Write a report and/or prepare a diagram explaining the relationship between the earth's axis and its orbit that causes these four "sun lines" to be located on the earth. (Reading about the **ecliptic** may be helpful.)

5. Historical parallels   For one or more of these events prepare a report naming the parallel that was involved and discussing why it was important. Attach a map locating the parallel.

   (a) The Korean War
   (b) The Vietnam War
   (c) The 1844 U.S. presidential election (President James Polk)
   (d) Mason and Dixon's Line
   (e) The Missouri Compromise, 1820

6. Important people   Write a report on one or more of these people, stressing the contributions to geography and navigation:

   (a) Bowditch, Nathaniel
   (b) Eratosthenes
   (c) Ptolemy
   (d) Sperry, Elmer
   (e) Strabo

Other projects:

Research 1:   Notes

The work in "Latitude Projects" can be used in a variety of ways. It can be strictly extra-credit; students may have complete freedom in choosing what to do and when to turn it in. Or it may be very structured; students can be assigned specific projects that are due on definite dates. Use this work in ways that best suit your situation, adding any appropriate projects and topics of your own.

Form   Be specific and clear on how students should prepare their projects. Cover these items: length; use of pencil, pen, or typing; use of only one or both sides of paper; inclusion of diagrams, maps, and illustrations; number and form of references. Stress also how the use of imagination can enhance reports and make them unique.

Library   Use these projects to help students develop library skills. Encourage thorough research. Scheduling class periods in the library is extremely helpful. Encourage students to go beyond encyclopedias as much as possible. This can involve the use of the card catalog, the table of contents and index of pertinent books, and the guides and indexes for appropriate periodicals. A constantly growing file of selected articles, maps, illustrations, diagrams, and clippings—referenced on subject cards in the card catalog— is a very valuable library feature for researching projects such as these.

Materials   The availability of certain materials in both the classroom and the library will be helpful for many students. If possible, have appropriate outline maps, tracing paper, and graph paper (helpful in making diagrams). Compasses, protractors, rulers, colored pencils, fine-point markers, and black-ink pens are also useful. Establish clear guidelines for the appropriate use and accountability of these materials.

Notes:

Activity G: Longitude—East or West

In Activity F you placed ten parallels on a grid to show the latitude, the location north or south, of ten places on earth. Now you will place ten vertical lines on the grid of Worksheet G to mark the east or west location of the same ten places. This measurement of an east or west location on the earth is called **longitude**. Lesson 4 on page 35 will discuss longitude in more detail.

A. Preparing the grid   Complete the grid on Worksheet G by neatly and carefully finishing the lettering or numbering of these items:

1. Title: LONGITUDE
2. 0° line: PRIME MERIDIAN
3. Directions: EAST, WEST
4. Scale labels: Degrees, East, West
5. Scale numbers: 0 to 180

B. Finding the locations   Use the scale and compass directions to find the location of the longitude of each of the ten places listed below. Use a straightedge to draw a dotted line at each longitude from the top to the bottom of the grid. Vertically label each dotted line near the bottom with the name and longitude of the place it locates.

1. Jakarta (Indonesia) . . . 107° E
2. Lima (Peru) . . . 77° W
3. Mexico City (Mexico) . . . 99° W
4. New Delhi (India) . . . 77° E
5. Nome (Alaska) . . . 165° W
6. Pretoria (South Africa) . . . 28° E
7. Seattle (Washington) . . . 122° W
8. South Georgia Island (South Atlantic Ocean) . . . 37° W
9. Tokyo (Japan) . . . 140° E
10. Wellington (New Zealand) . . . 175° E

Note: Do not put the information in parentheses on your grid. It is given simply to help you know in a general way where each place is.

If this longitude grid were combined with the latitude grid from Activity F, intersecting lines would indicate the exact location of each of the ten places. After learning a little more about longitude, you will be completing a grid that does show precisely "where on earth" these ten places are.

Where on Earth? Understanding Latitude and Longitude

Name: _____   Date: _____   *32S*

Worksheet G: Grid

LO _ _ _ _ _ _

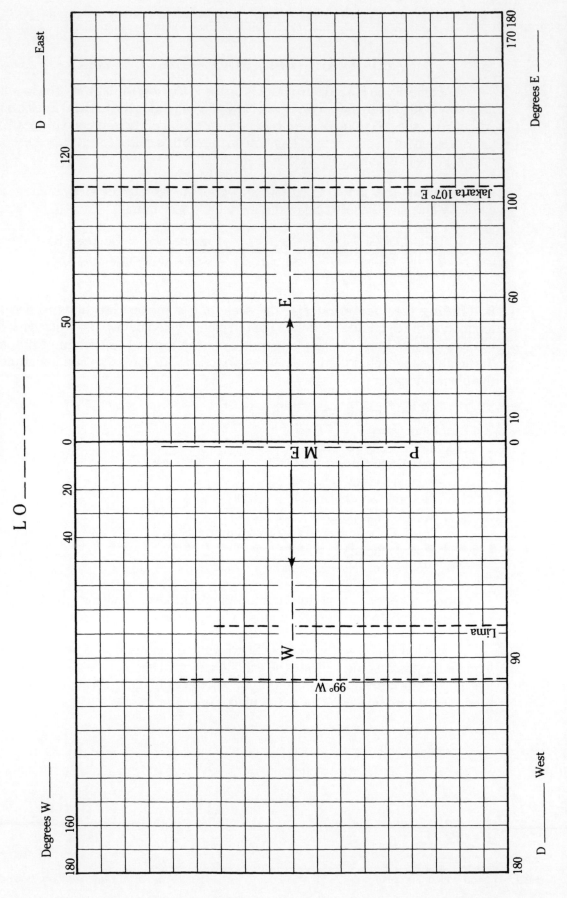

Degrees W _____   Degrees E _____

West   East

© 1989 J. Weston Walch, Publisher   *Where on Earth? Understanding Latitude and Longitude*

Activity G: Notes

Both the instruction sheet and the worksheet need to be handed out for Activity G. Remind students to read the directions carefully and to work slowly in order to produce a good grid. Discuss the tools—fine-point marker, soft eraser, straightedge, etc.—that are needed for this work.

Caution students that space for the numbers identifying the lines is limited. Some students may be skilled at staggering the numbers or writing them vertically. The best method for most, however, will be to number every other line by 20s. The important thing is that these line labels be neat and clear.

Insist that students read the directions carefully and study the work already done on the grid before they are given any individual help. It is important that they learn to work independently. Tell students that no second worksheets will be given out. If they damage theirs with errors, they will have to make a complete new one on $\frac{1}{4}$-inch graph paper. It is also important that they learn to work accurately.

Key The key along the margin of Worksheet G on page 34T should help in checking papers quickly. Allow for some variation in the location of the dotted lines because of the estimating required between grid lines. Consider neatness and completeness as well as accuracy in grading papers.

Visual Make overhead transparencies of good student grids. Have their makers show them to the class to explain how they were produced and to demonstrate how they can be interpreted. Grade students on the quality of these presentations.

Enrichment Some of the differences between latitude and longitude can be demonstrated by slicing an orange and an apple for the class. Slice the orange to show the parallels, or lines of latitude, by cutting across the axis. If the first cut is across the center, it can demonstrate the equator, a great circle, and the northern and southern hemispheres. Cut the apple into wedges to illustrate the meridians, or lines of longitude. The first cut can show the prime meridian, a great circle, the poles, the axis, and the eastern and western hemispheres. This demonstration can be made more effective by using larger items such as grapefruit or melons and by first putting grid lines on the surface with a marker. A globe for comparisons will also help students visualize what is going on.

Notes:

Activity G: Key

LONGITUDE

Degrees East

Degrees East

180 170 160 150 140 130 120 110 100 90 80 70 60 50 40 30 20 10 0 10 20 30 40 50 60 70 80 90 100 110 120 130 140 150 160 170 180

Wellington 175° E

Tokyo 140° E

Jakarta 107° E

New Delhi 77° E

EAST

Pretoria 28° E

PRIME MERIDIAN

South Georgia Island 37° W

WEST

Lima 77° W

Mexico City 99° W

Seattle 122° W

Nome 165° W

Degrees West

Degrees West

180 170 160 150 140 130 120 110 100 90 80 70 60 50 40 30 20 10 0 10 20 30 40 50 60 70 80 90 100 110 120 130 140 150 160 170 180

West

Nome 165° W

Seattle 122° W

Mexico City 99° W

Lima 77° W

South Georgia Island 37° W

Pretoria 28° E

New Delhi 77° E

Jakarta 107° E

Tokyo 140° E

Wellington 175° E

East

Where on Earth? Understanding Latitude and Longitude

Lesson 4:   What Is Longitude?

Basically, **longitude** is how far east or west from a certain point a place is located. There is a need to be exact with earth locations, though, so a good definition of longitude should be more precise.

To be more exact, **longitude is the angular distance due east or west from the prime meridian (Greenwich Meridian) of a location on the earth.**

The polar view of the earth in this diagram will help you understand longitude. **Angular distance** means that longitude, like latitude, is expressed as the number of degrees in an angle of the spherical earth. If you have problems with this concept, refer to Lesson 2 on page 17S.

Due east or west means that longitude measurements are always made along straight lines that travel in a true east or west direction. This means that as the longitude measurement goes from the 0° line, it is perpendicular to that line and forms right angles with it. The longitude measurement then continues east or west in a straight line to the place it locates.

Finally, **from the prime meridian (Greenwich Meridian)** tells us that the starting point for measuring longitude is an imaginary north-south line (meridian) running from the North Pole to the South Pole and passing through Greenwich, England. The earth does not have a natural north-south "sun line" that can serve as the zero line for longitude as the equator does for latitude. Therefore, a world conference in 1884 agreed that the meridian of the Greenwich Observatory, located in a section of London, England, would be the starting point for measurements of longitude. It is at 0° longitude. As locations move east or west from the Greenwich Meridian, the number of degrees indicating their longitude gets larger.

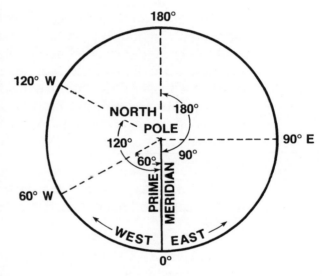

Where on Earth? Understanding Latitude and Longitude

Lesson 4:   What Is Longitude? *(continued)*

How high can a reading of longitude go? Since longitude measurements in one compass direction go halfway around the world, they range from 0° at the prime meridian to 180° at the meridian 180 degrees away. With the exception of these two readings, all longitude measurements must have the direction *east* or *west* given with the number of degrees.

On maps and globes, longitude measurements are represented by north-south lines called **meridians**. Meridians are imaginary straight lines running from the North Pole to the South Pole. (In Activity G you located the meridians for ten places.) A place on earth with a given longitude will be found somewhere along the meridian that marks that longitude.

Of the two measurements you are studying, latitude was the easiest for early travelers to determine. Rough estimates of it could be made without the use of instruments by judging the North Star's angle above the horizon. But longitude could only be determined accurately by comparing the time at one's present location to the time at the point from which one had started. For example, if a traveler with the noon sun overhead had a clock that showed the time at his departure point as midnight, he would know he had gone halfway around the world, or 180 degrees. The development of this accurate, portable timepiece, however, was a slow, difficult process. A reliable one, the **chronometer**, was not perfected until the late 1700s.

Definitions   Use a dictionary to find the meanings of the eight words below as they apply to longitude and directions. Do these activities as directed by your teacher:

(a) On a separate sheet of paper, write a complete, accurate definition of each word.

(b) Use each word correctly in a good sentence.

(c) Be prepared to report orally on the pronunciation, meaning, and use of the words.

1. chronometer	5. longitude
2. due (adv.)	6. meridian (n.)
3. great circle	7. prime (adj.)
4. Greenwich Meridian	8. prime meridian

Where on Earth? Understanding Latitude and Longitude

Lesson 4:   Notes and Answers

For "What Is Longitude?" a thorough oral reading and discussion are recommended to ensure student understanding. Refer to the diagram and use an overhead projector, a world wall map, and a globe for reinforcement. In discussions try to use Definitions words from both this lesson and the previous ones.

Definitions   Be sure students know which activities are to be done. Remind them to note part-of-speech abbreviations and to keep definitions relevant.

1. chronometer
    (a) an extremely accurate timepiece
    (b) The navigator uses a *chronometer* to determine his longitude.

2. due (adv.)
    (a) in a straight line; exactly
    (b) The plane flew *due* east of the airport.

3. great circle
    (a) a circle on the earth that passes directly over the earth's center
    (b) The shortest air route follows a *great circle*.

4. Greenwich Meridian
    (a) the meridian of Greenwich, England; starting point for measuring longitude
    (b) The prime meridian for measurements of longitude is the *Greenwich Meridian*.

5. longitude
    (a) the angular distance due east or west from the prime meridian (Greenwich Meridian) of a location on the earth
    (b) the *longitude* at Greenwich, England, is 0° .

6. meridian (n.)
    (a) an imaginary north-south line running from pole to pole, used to measure longitude
    (b) *Meridians* are also known as lines of longitude.

7. prime (adj.)
    (a) first; main
    (b) A drought was the *prime* reason for the famine.

8. prime meridian
    (a) the meridian at 0° longitude; the Greenwich Meridian; starting point for measuring longitude
    (b) The *prime meridian* passes through parts of Europe and Africa.

Research 2:   Longitude Projects

Do any of these projects as your teacher may direct for regular class assignments or extra-credit work. Do your best to produce neat, well-organized material.

1. Great circles Write a report on **great circles** and their use in **great-circle routes** for ships and planes. Use diagrams and/or maps to illustrate your report. Also prepare a chart comparing distances between various places on the earth as determined by using the scale on first a world map and then a globe. Use the scale carefully. Copying and extending it on the edge of a piece of paper makes a useful tool for determining distances.

2. Air-travel pioneers   Read and report on the book *North to the Orient* by Anne Morrow Lindbergh. Include a map of the flight and explain how it relates to great-circle routes. Also read about Charles Lindbergh and describe his work in introducing air travel to the world.

3. Where days begin Prepare a report that names and describes the imaginary irregular line that runs from the North Pole to the South Pole on or near the 180-degree meridian. Describe what happens to travelers who cross it. Illustrate your report with a map and/or diagram. Explain the necessity for this interesting line. A north polar map that shows the 24 time zones labeled by hour *and* day will help this explanation.

4. Yours or mine?   Write a report on the **Line of Demarcation** of 1493–94. Mention who helped establish it and why. Describe some of its effects and include a map showing its location.

5. Potpourri   Prepare a report on one or more of these subjects. Include suitable maps, diagrams, or illustrations.

   (a) chronometer

   (b) Cook, James

   (c) Greenwich time, Royal Greenwich Observatory

   (d) Harrison, John

   (e) nautical miles, knot, statute miles

   (f) sundial

Where on Earth? Understanding Latitude and Longitude

Research 2:   Longitude Projects *(continued)*

6. Time zones   Prepare a report explaining why 15 degrees is a common interval between meridians on many world maps. Start your research by dividing the number of degrees in a circle by the number of hours in a day. Give the general name for this area of 15 degrees and the specific names for these four areas of the mainland United States. Include United States and/or world maps that illustrate these 15-degree "zones." Explain why the boundaries of the zones sometimes zigzag.

7. Directions in names   Prepare an outline world map that locates and names some of the many places on the earth that use a compass direction as a part of their name. Use symbols and a key if necessary. Here are some names to help you get started:

(a) East Indies

(b) Eastern Europe

(c) The Midwest (U.S.)

(d) Near East

(e) Northwest Passage

(f) South Pacific Ocean

8. Boundary lines   Prepare an outline map of the United States to show the many parallels and meridians that serve as state boundary lines. Darken these boundaries and indicate their latitude or longitude reading.

9. Meridians and time   Write a report on the meaning of **meridian, a.m.**, and **p.m.** Look up these terms in an unabridged dictionary so you can discuss their etymology (history). Describe thoroughly how **a.m.** and **p.m.** are used and illustrate your report with diagrams.

Other projects:

Where on Earth? Understanding Latitude and Longitude

Research 2:   Notes

The activities in "Longitude Projects" are designed to broaden student understanding of earth locations and to develop their research and study skills. Use them in ways that best suit you and your classes. Some projects may serve as an assignment for the entire class. Others will work best as extra-credit material. Add activities and subjects of your own to enrich this work.

Preparing well for work on projects will help students do a good job. Review the ideas presented on page 30T. Remind students of the importance of allowing adequate time, doing complete research, and producing neat work. Review the report form to be used as well as the available ways to use the library.

Oral work   Presenting projects as oral reports to the class is a valuable experience for students. Prepare classes for this work by providing guidelines for oral presentations. These can be listed on individual handout sheets or on posters or chalkboards. Whatever the printed form, have a thorough oral review of the guidelines with each class. Here are some suggestions for good oral presentations:

1. Prepare well. Do good research. Speak from notes on cards. Read the presentation only if you have to.

2. Use some large type of visual device. This may be a graph, map, chart, diagram, illustration, or model.

3. Practice and time your presentation. Be familiar with it and know it is the right length, _____ minutes.

4. Use good posture, eye contact, and voice projection. Be a serious, interesting speaker before the class and a polite, interested listener in the audience.

Enrichment   Review how latitude and longitude use the idea of *due* with compass directions by locating a few points on a world wall map. To find a latitude, go *due* north or south on a meridian, probably the prime meridian, to the proper latitude. To find a longitude, go *due* east or west on a parallel, probably the equator, to the correct longitude. Point out that latitude and longitude are *straight* measurements along the four cardinal points. They do not go off in any direction; they go *due* north, south, east, or west. The best way to observe this is to follow the grid lines—the parallels and meridians—when locating latitude or longitude.

Notes:

Name: _____ Date: _____ *41S*

Activity H: Between the Lines

If the parallels and meridians for all possible locations were drawn on maps, the maps would be covered solid with lines. Instead, a few parallels and meridians are placed at regular intervals, often of 10 or 15 degrees. *Estimating* degrees between these lines is required to locate most latitudes and longitudes. Use this activity to sharpen your estimating skills.

Directions   Complete the grid labels with the correct missing numbers and letters. Then give the full latitude and longitude reading for each dot on the map.

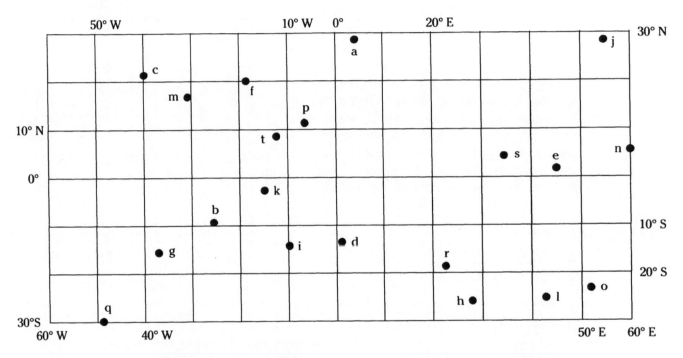

	Latitude	Longitude		Latitude	Longitude
a.	29° N	4° E	k.	_____	_____
b.	9° S	_____	l.	_____	_____
c.	_____	40° W	m.	_____	_____
d.	_____	_____	n.	_____	_____
e.	_____	_____	o.	_____	_____
f.	_____	_____	p.	_____	_____
g.	_____	_____	q.	_____	_____
h.	_____	_____	r.	_____	_____
i.	_____	_____	s.	_____	_____
j.	_____	_____	t.	_____	_____

Where on Earth? Understanding Latitude and Longitude

Activity H: Notes and Answers

Caution students to label the "Between the Lines" grid carefully. Each grid number should have the degree symbol, as on a real map. Real map grids do not include the compass direction initial with each number. However, these initials are included on this drill to ensure that students know the directions. If longitude labels are too crowded, most of their direction initials may be omitted. Tell students to memorize the cardinal points on a standard map—north to the top, etc.—if they do not already know them.

Visual Use this diagram on a chalkboard or as an overhead transparency to help students understand estimating. The dotted lines and their values must be imagined on a real grid. Point out to students that the compass directions —though not labeled—may be easily determined by noting in which direction the numbers get larger. Be sure that both the word *degree* and the compass direction are given as part of the latitude and longitude in this drill.

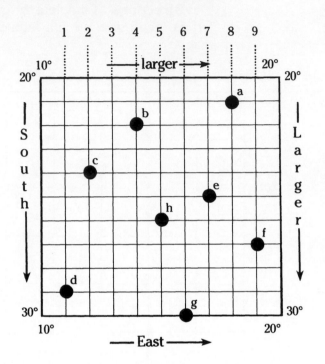

Answers:

a.	21° S, 18° E;	e.	25° S, 17° E;
b.	22° S, 14° E;	f.	27° S, 19° E;
c.	24° S, 12° E;	g.	30° S, 16° E;
d.	29° S, 11° E;	h.	26° S, 15° E;

Answers The number, degree symbol, and compass direction initial are all needed for a correct answer. An error of one degree should be allowed for estimating.

	Latitude	Longitude		Latitude	Longitude
a.	29° N	4° E	k.	3° S	16° W
b.	9° S	25° W	l.	25° S	43° E
c.	22° N	40° W	m.	17° N	31° W
d.	13° S	1° E	n.	6.° N	60° E
e.	2° N	46° E	o.	23° S	52° E
f.	20° N	19° W	p.	11° N	7° W
g.	16° S	37° W	q.	30° S	49° W
h.	26° S	28° E	r.	19° S	22° E
i.	14° S	10° W	s.	5° N	34° E
j.	28° N	55° E	t.	8° N	13° W

Activity I: Latitude and Longitude

In Activities F and G you indicated the latitude and longitude of ten places on earth by drawing dotted lines to indicate their parallels and meridians. On the grid of Worksheet I, you will combine these two steps by showing the precise location of each of these ten places with a dot. Your completed grid will thus come closer to resembling a true world map.

A. Preparing the grid   Use a straightedge to complete the rectangle and two center lines of the grid on Worksheet I. Then neatly and carefully finish lettering or numbering these items:

1. Title: LATITUDE AND LONGITUDE
2. Center lines: Equator, Greenwich Meridian
3. Directions: Longitude West of Greenwich, Longitude East of Greenwich
4. Numbers: 0° to 90° , 0° to 180° (Stagger or omit some longitude numbers to avoid crowding.)

B. Finding the locations   Use latitude and longitude to place a dot on the grid to show the location of each of the ten places listed below. Label each dot with the name of the place it locates. *Do not* write the latitude and longitude readings by the names. Use estimating to get each dot as close to the correct location as possible.

1. Jakarta (Indonesia)	6° S . . 107° E
2. Lima (Peru)	12° S . . 77° W
3. Mexico City (Mexico)	19° N . . 99° W
4. New Delhi (India)	29° N . . 77° E
5. Nome (Alaska)	65° N . . 165° W
6. Pretoria (South Africa)	26° S . . 28° E
7. Seattle (Washington)	48° N . . 122° W
8. South Georgia Island (South Atlantic Ocean)	54° S . . 37° W
9. Tokyo (Japan)	36° N . . 140° E
10. Wellington (New Zealand)	41° S . . 175° E

Note: Do not put the information in parentheses on your grid. It is given simply to help you know in a general way where each place is.

Your completed grid and a comparable world map should show each place in approximately the same location. If there are large differences, check your work, particularly the compass directions. For minor differences see if variations in the two grids account for small changes in location.

Where on Earth? Understanding Latitude and Longitude

Name: _____

Date: _____

Worksheet I: Grid

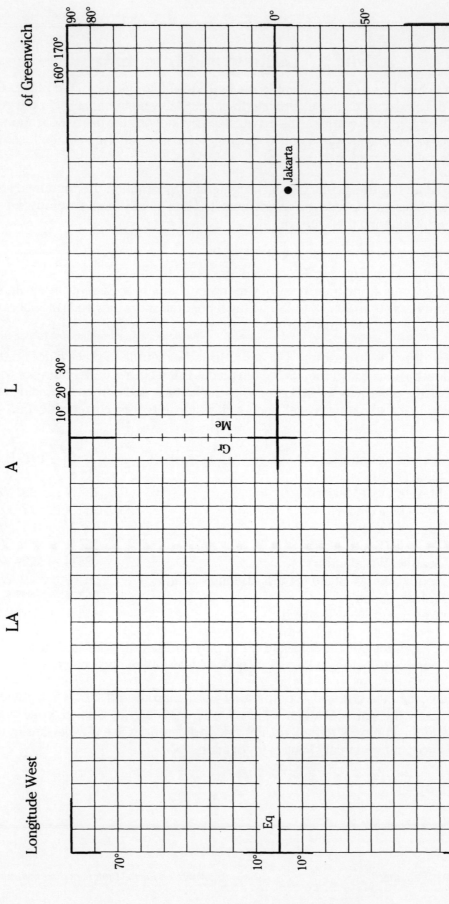

LA

A

L

Longitude West

of Greenwich

Where on Earth? Understanding Latitude and Longitude

Activity I: Notes

Tell students to read the directions for Activity I very carefully. The labeling and numbering are different from the earlier grids and are more like those found on real maps. Point out that graph paper lines are helpful guides for neat letters and numbers. If students find their longitude numbers are too crowded, tell them to stagger them or number every other meridian by 20s. Remind students that estimating is required to place dots accurately. Some may want to use a straightedge, which may simply be the edge of a piece of paper, to "hold" or "remember" one coordinate line on the grid while they locate the other.

Checking student grids takes time, but is very important. Reliable students can help—and also learn—in this process. The marginal keys from Activities F and G can speed checking by being aligned with this Activity I grid and then slowly moved over it.

Visual Put this diagram and the chart below on the chalkboard to help students learn how to locate points with latitude and longitude more quickly and accurately. Help students see the similarity between the diagram, the grid, and a world map. Point out how the two compass directions of the coordinates tell in which quarter of the map a location will be found.

Northwest	Greenwich Meridian	Northeast
Equator		
Southwest		Southeast

Latitude	Longitude	World Map Quarter
North	East	Northeast (Upper Right)
North	West	Northwest (Upper Left)
South	East	Southeast (Lower Right)
South	West	Southwest (Lower Left)

Notes:

Activity I: Key

LATITUDE AND LONGITUDE

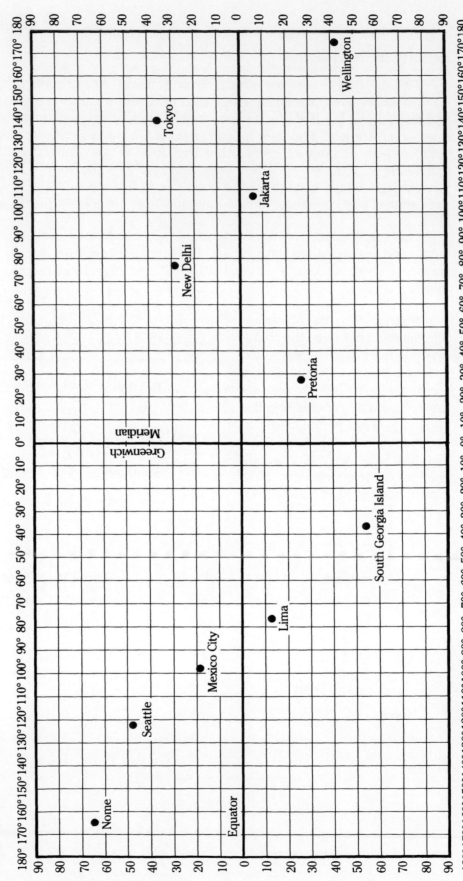

Longitude East of Greenwich

Longitude West of Greenwich

Activity J: Ten More Places

This activity introduces the idea of **relative location**, which involves describing a place not just as a spot where two lines cross, but as a place relating to other things. Follow directions carefully and work neatly as you locate *and describe* "Ten More Places" on earth.

A. Preparing the grid   Use a straightedge to complete the rectangle and two center lines of the grid on Worksheet J. Then neatly and carefully finish lettering and numbering these items:

1. Title: TEN MORE PLACES
2. Center Lines: Equator, Greenwich Meridian
3. Directions: Longitude West of Greenwich, Longitude East of Greenwich
4. Numbers: 0° to 90° , 0° to 180° (Stagger or omit some longitude numbers to avoid crowding.)

B. Locating and describing   On the grid locate each of the ten places below with a dot labeled with that place's name. After each place name below write a good sentence describing that place's relationship to some other thing(s) on earth. Example: New York City is on the east coast of the United States. You will need to refer to a world map or atlas for this work.

1. Cairo . . 30° N . . 31° E Cairo is located at the mouth of the _____ River.

2. Canton . . 23° N . . 113° E _____

    _____

3. Honolulu . . 21° N . . 158° W _____

    _____

4. Lake Victoria . . 1° S . . 33° E _____

    _____

5. London . . 52° N . . 0° _____

    _____

6. Melbourne . . 38° S . . 145° E _____

    _____

7. Montreal . . 46° N . . 74° W _____

    _____

8. San Francisco . . 38° N . . 122° W _____

    _____

9. Santiago . . 33° S . . 71° W _____

    _____

10. Tahiti . . 18° S . . 150° W _____

    _____

Name: _____   Date: _____

Worksheet J: Grid

T   M   P

of Greenwich   Longitude East

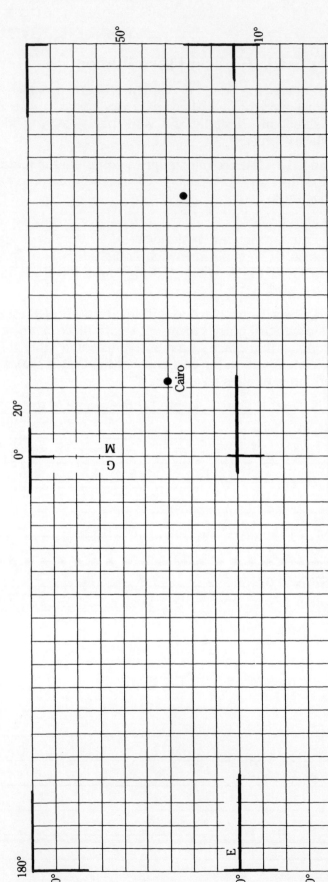

Where on Earth? Understanding Latitude and Longitude

Activity J: Notes and Answers

"Ten More Places" should be introduced by briefly discussing how a location may be both *absolute* and *relative*. The grid location, using latitude and longitude, is mechanical and precise; it is an *absolute location. Relative location* describes a place in terms of what it is a part of, what is nearby, and what interactions occur. Discussing relative location brings geography alive with physical and cultural dynamics.

Be sure students have access to atlases or maps from which they can get information for describing the ten places. Caution them to use proper mechanics and spelling when writing the sentences. Encourage students to be perceptive and imaginative in developing descriptions. On a map, for example, keys indicate capital cities; countries controlling islands are named; and nearby rivers, mountains, and oceans are shown.

Answers   Correctness of grammar and spelling, as well as geographic accuracy, should be considered in evaluating student sentences. Review this work orally, with students reading some of their own descriptions, to expose classes to good examples. Offer samples yourself, using a world wall map to illustrate various relative locations. These sentences are possible answers:

1. Cairo is located at the mouth of the Nile River.
2. Canton is on the coast of southeastern China.
3. Honolulu is a city in the island state of Hawaii.
4. Lake Victoria lies along the equator in eastern Africa.
5. London is the capital city of the United Kingdom.
6. Melbourne is on the Australian coast near the island of Tasmania.
7. Montreal, Canada, is on the Saint Lawrence River.
8. San Francisco is on the Pacific coast of the United States.
9. Santiago, the capital of Chile, is on South America's west coast.
10. Tahiti is an island in the South Pacific Ocean.

Notes:

Activity J: Key

TEN MORE PLACES

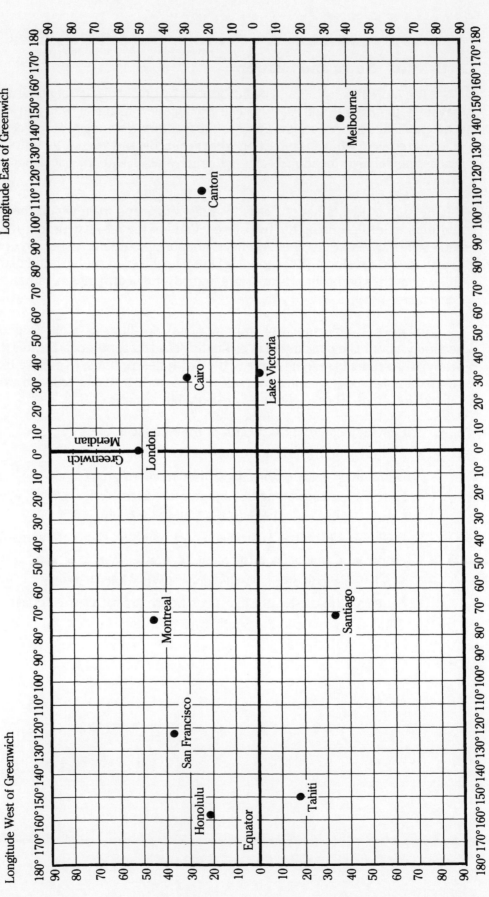

Longitude West of Greenwich

Longitude East of Greenwich

Where on Earth? Understanding Latitude and Longitude

Activity K: Mercator Map I

Worksheet K has a world map designed by Gerhardus Mercator, a Belgian mapmaker of the 1500s. Because its parallels and meridians are straight lines, its grid closely resembles the ones with which you have been working. Note that toward the poles the parallels get farther apart, but the interval of ten degrees stays the same. Your worksheet map shows the landmasses most used by humans, so more of the northern hemisphere is included and the polar areas are omitted.

A. Preparing the map   Complete the map on Worksheet K by neatly and carefully finishing the lettering or numbering of these items.:

1. Title: MERCATOR MAP I
2. Directions: Longitude West of Greenwich, Longitude East of Greenwich
3. Numbers: 0° to 70°, 0° to 60°, 0° to 180° (Follow your teacher's suggestions to avoid crowding longitude numbers.)

B. Finding the locations   Use latitude and longitude to place a dot on the map to show the location of each of the fifteen places listed below. Label each dot with the name of the place it locates. Use careful *estimating*, map *quarters*, and a *straightedge* memory for accurate work.

1. Buenos Aires	34° S . .	59° W
2. Cairo	30° N . .	31° E
3. Denver	40° N . .	105° W
4. Honolulu	21° N . .	158° W
5. Lima	12° S . .	77° W
6. London	52° N . .	0°
7. Montreal	46° N . .	74° W
8. New Delhi	29° N . .	77° E
9. Pretoria	26° S . .	28° E
10. Santiago	33° S . .	71° W
11. South Georgia Island	54° S . .	37° W
12. Sydney	34° S . .	151° E
13. Vladivostok	43° N . .	132° E
14. Warsaw	52° N . .	21° E
15. Wellington	41° S . .	175° E

Where on Earth? Understanding Latitude and Longitude

Name: _____

Date: _____

Worksheet K: Map

L ____ W ____ G ____ M ____ M ____ I ____ E

52S

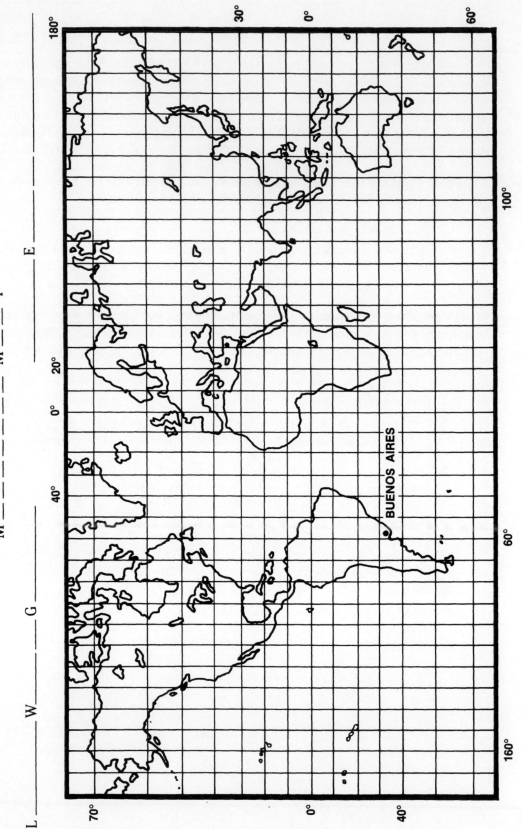

BUENOS AIRES

Where on Earth? Understanding Latitude and Longitude

Activity K: Notes

As students start on Mercator Map I, discuss various ways to avoid crowding the numbers that identify the meridians. Some students can write numbers small enough to fit. Others may elect to stagger the numbers so they overlap slightly. The best way for many students will be to label every other meridian, counting by 20s. The key on page 54T illustrates these three techniques. Emphasize that students shouldd be neat and accurate in whatever numbering method they choose, for the usefulness of any map depends upon the clarity of all its labels.

Stress again the importance of working first in pencil, then using pen or fine-point marker. The dots locating the places should be easy to see, but not overly large. The name identifying each dot should be printed legibly near the dot. The map—as well as student understanding of the world—will be helped if colored pencils are used to *lightly* shade the water blue and the land brown or green. Have students refer to an atlas if necessary and work carefully; distinguishing water from land can be difficult in certain areas.

Enrichment As students now start to use latitude and longitude to locate places on real maps, review some skills needed in using map grids. The cardinal points on a world map are critical. Point them out on a world wall map and drill students so they automatically know north is up, east to the right, and so on. Also discuss and demonstrate these techniques:

1. **Estimating** On the chalkboard use a diagram similar to the one on page 42T. Review that the compass directions are determined by the direction in which the degrees get larger. Have students estimate the latitude and longitude of various dots placed in the square.

2. **Quarters** Point out the four map quarters—northeast, southeast, etc.—on a world wall map. Have students indicate which map quarter they would search to find places for which you give the coordinates.

3. **Straightedge** Have two students use a yardstick to show how a straightedge "holds" one coordinate on a wall map while the other coordinate is located. Have one student hold the stick at a given latitude to "remember" it while the second student finds the longitude and follows it to the yardstick for the correct location.

Notes:

Activity K: Key

<u>MERCATOR MAP I</u>

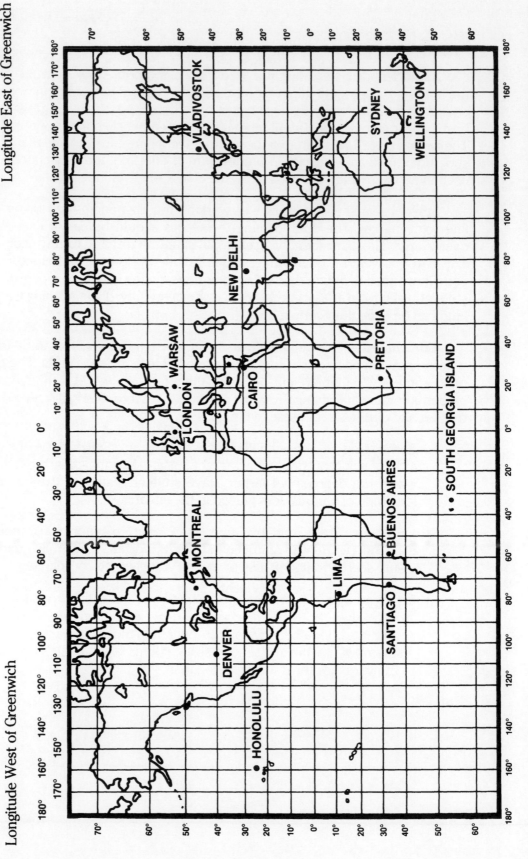

Longitude East of Greenwich

Longitude West of Greenwich

Where on Earth? Understanding Latitude and Longitude

Activity L: Mercator Map II

A. Preparing the map   Complete the map on Worksheet L by neatly and carefully finishing the lettering or numbering of these items:

1. Title: MERCATOR MAP II
2. Directions: Longitude West of Greeenwich, Longitude East of Greenwich
3. Numbers: 0° to 70° , 0° to 60° , 0° to 180° (Avoid crowding the longitude numbers.)

B. Locating and describing   On the map locate each of the fifteen places below with a dot labeled with that place's name. For each of the ten names below followed by blanks write a good sentence describing that place's relationship to some other thing(s) on earth. Use a world map or atlas for this work.

1. Aral Sea . . 45° N . . 60° E The Aral Sea is an inland sea in the south-western Soviet _____ . _____

2. Brasilia . . 16° S . . 48° W _____

   _____

3. Canton . . 23° N . .113° E

4. Chicago . . 41° N . .88° W _____

   _____

5. Falkland Islands . . 51° S . .61° W _____

   _____

6. Jakarta . .6° S . . 107° E _____

   _____

7. Lake Victoria . . 1° S . . 33° E
8. Melbourne . . 38° S . . 145° E
9. Mexico City . . 19° N . . 99° W _____

   _____

10. Nome . . 65° N . .165° W _____

    _____

11. Rome . . 42° N . .13° E _____

    _____

12. Seattle . .48° N . .122° W _____

    _____

13. Tahiti . . 18° S . . 150° W
14. Antananarivo . . 19° S . . 48° E
15. Tokyo . . 36° N . . 140° E _____

    _____

Where on Earth? Understanding Latitude and Longitude

Name: _____

Date: _____

56S

Worksheet L: Map

M ___ ___ ___ I ___ M ___ ___ ___ E ___ G

L ___ ___ ___ W ___ G

ARAL SEA

Where on Earth? Understanding Latitude and Longitude

© 1989 J. Weston Walch, Publisher

Activity L: Notes and Answers

Be sure students have access to maps or atlases for this work. Encourage them to write more precise descriptions by using large-scale maps in an atlas to obtain more detailed information. They can do this by first applying the latitude and longitude readings to a world map to find the nation, continent, or ocean in which the place is located. Then they can use the table of contents to find the more detailed regional map showing the relative location of the place they want to describe.

Encourage students to incorporate more than one relative location in their sentences. Compass directions are easy to include, as are the relationships to bodies of water. A valuable writing technique for "sneaking in" an additional relationship is the use of the appositive.

Answers   Use plenty of classroom discussion and chalkboard examples to expose students to sentences that illustrate complete, well-written descriptions. These sentences illustrate possible answers:

1. The Aral Sea is an inland sea in the southwestern Soviet Union.

2. Brazil's capital, Brasilia, is located in the nation's interior.

4. Chicago is in northeast Illinois, at the southern end of Lake Michigan.

5. Although governed by the United Kingdom, the Falkland Islands lie near the southern tip of South America.

6. The capital of Indonesia, Jakarta, is located on the island of Java.

9. Mexico's capital, Mexico City, is in the central part of the country.

10. Nome is on Alaska's west coast, close to the Soviet Union.

11. Rome, the capital of Italy, is centered on its western coast.

12. Seattle is a large city on Puget Sound in western Washington.

15. Tokyo, Japan's capital city, is on the Pacific coast of the island of Honshu.

Notes:

Activity L: Key

MERCATOR MAP II

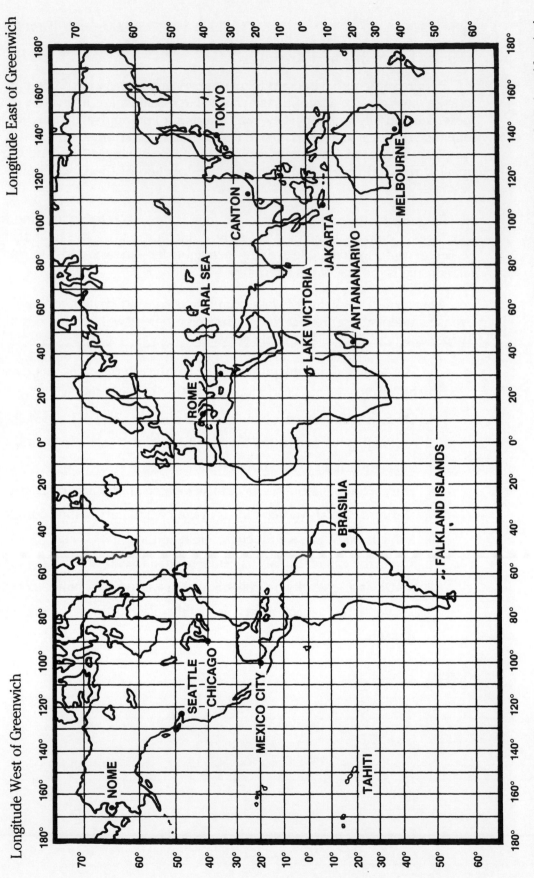

Longitude West of Greenwich

Longitude East of Greenwich

Where on Earth? Understanding Latitude and Longitude

Lesson 5:   Map Projections

In Activities M and N you will notice that the world map is different from the Mercator map you have been using. You have probably already noticed differences between other world maps that you have seen and used. These different kinds of maps result from the fact that there are various ways to show the surface of the curved earth on flat paper. These different methods of showing all or part of the earth's curving surface on a flat map are called **projections**.

Projecting the earth's curving surface onto flat paper is not an easy job. It involves the use of complicated mathematics and geometry that can produce numerous kinds of projections. There is a huge, often confusing variety of names for all these projections. For example, a projection may be named for the cartographer who invented it, for the system used to make it, or for the appearance of the final map. If you look closely, you will usually find the projection's name somewhere on most maps you use.

One way to name map projections comes from the relationship between the flat map and the spherical globe. A **plane** projection keeps the map flat and touches it to the globe at one point. A polar map uses this kind of projection. A **conic** projection forms the map into a cone and sets it on the globe. Maps of the United States are commonly made with this projection. A **cylindrical** projection wraps the map around the globe as a cylinder. The Mercator map results from this technique.

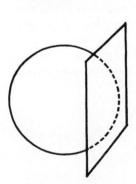

Plane Projection

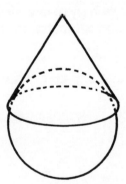

Conic Projection

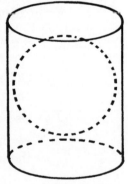

Cylindrical Projection

Another way of naming projections describes their appearance. An **interrupted** projection omits wedge-shaped pieces of the map. The resulting map gives the feeling that the earth's surface was "peeled" off the globe. An **elliptical** projection, the one that will be used in Activities M and N, has an oval shape. Many

Where on Earth? Understanding Latitude and Longitude

Lesson 5:   Map Projections *(continued)*

world maps use forms of this projection because it reduces the **distortion**, or loss of accuracy, in the polar areas that occurs on a Mercator map.

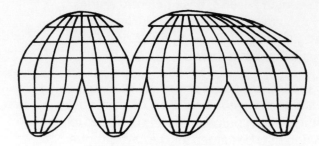

Interrupted Projection

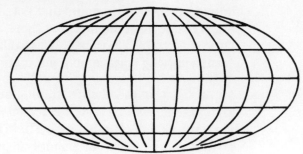

Elliptical Projection

Distortion occurs in all maps because the curved surface of the earth ends up being stretched and pulled when shown on a flat map. Cartographers just can't make a map that is accurate in all properties such as shape, distance, and area. In obtaining accuracy in one property such as shape, they might settle for distortion in distance or area. Today computer technology, satellite data, and aerial photography provide much information for many types of maps. Mapmakers, however, must still decide which of the many available map projections will represent this material in the most accurate and useful form.

Definitions   Use a dictionary to find the meanings of the six words below as they apply to mapmaking and geometry. Do these activities as directed by your teacher:

(a) On a separate sheet of paper, write a complete, accurate definition of each word.

(b) Use each word correctly in a good sentence.

(c) Be prepared to report orally on the pronunciation, meaning, and use of the words.

    1. cone (n.)   4. ellipse

    2. cylinder   5. plane (n.)

    3. distortion   6. projection

Lesson 5: Notes and Answers

The three general types of map projections discussed in Lesson 5 should help students visualize what map projection means. Their understanding will be helped if the material is read aloud, thoroughly discussed, and illustrated on the chalkboard. Tell students that there truly are numerous map projections filling various needs and bearing names ranging from the "responsible-cartographer" (Mercator) to the "accurate-property" (equal-area).

Use a globe and a piece of heavy paper to demonstrate the three projections; illustrate their resulting maps with wall maps. Have students compare the two outline world maps—Mercator, page 56S, and elliptical, page 63S—to note differences and similarities.

Definitions   Be sure students know which activities are to be done. Remind them to note part-of-speech abbreviations and to keep definitions relevant. Suggest that more understandable definitions of geometric figures will be found in more elementary dictionaries. Also point out how challenging it is to define some of these figures in words only and how illustrations can clarify the definitions.

1. cone (n.)
   (a) a figure with a round, flat base at one end and straight sides tapering to a point at the other end
   (b) A witch's hat is shaped like a *cone*.

2. cylinder
   (a) a figure with a circular cross section and straight sides extending to flat ends.
   (b) A tin can has the shape of a *cylinder*.

3. distortion
   (a) a twisting, bending, or pulling out of shape
   (b) A Mercator map does not have *distortion* along the equator.

4. ellipse
   (a) a flat figure shaped like an oval
   (b) The stadium was built in the form of an *ellipse*.

5. plane (n.)
   (a) a perfectly flat surface, often imagined
   (b) The *plane* of the equator divides the earth in half.

6. projection
   (a) one of the many methods used to represent the earth's curved surface on a flat map
   (b) A conic *projection* is often used for maps of the United States.

Notes:

Activity M: Elliptical Map I

Worksheet M uses a world map made from an elliptical projection. Because it stresses land masses most used by humans, the polar areas are limited and more of the northern hemisphere is shown. The parallels are straight lines, but the meridians curve toward the poles, creating a feeling of roundness. Even though the parallels get farther apart near the poles, their interval is always ten degrees. But work with longitude very carefully! The meridians have an interval of *fifteen* degrees. They are sometimes placed this way on world maps to mark the twenty-four time zones.

A. Preparing the map   Complete the map on Worksheet M by neatly and carefully finishing the lettering or numbering of these items:

1. Title: ELLIPTICAL MAP I
2. Directions: Longitude West of Greenwich, Longitude East of Greenwich
3. Numbers: 0° to 80° , 0° to 70° , 0° to 180° (Avoid crowding the longitude numbers.)

B. Finding the locations   Use latitude and longitude to place a dot on the map to show the location of each of the fifteen places listed below. Label each dot with the name of the place it locates. Use careful *estimating*, map *quarters*, and a *straightedge* memory for accurate work.

1.	Barrow	71° N . . 156° W
2.	Brasilia	16° S . . 48° W
3.	Buenos Aires	34° S . . 59° W
4.	Canton	23° N . . 113° E
5.	Casablanca	34° N . . 8° W
6.	Chicago	41° N . . 88° W
7.	Hobart	43° S . . 148° E
8.	Montreal	46° N . . 74° W
9.	Paris	49° N . . 2° E
10.	Phoenix	34° N . . 112° W
11.	Santiago	33° S . . 71° W
12.	Tahiti	18° S . . 150° W
13.	Antananarivo	19° S . . 48° E
14.	Vladivostok	43° N . . 132° E
15.	Wellington	41° S . . 175° E

Where on Earth? Understanding Latitude and Longitude

Name: _____

Date: _____

Worksheet M: Map

E _____

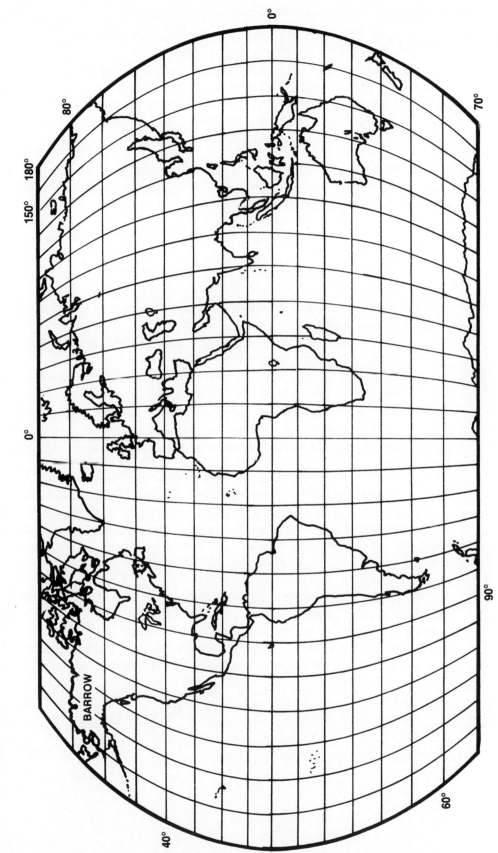

0°

80°

180°

150°

0°

70°

90°

60°

40°

BARROW

Activity M: Notes

Even though the top and the bottom parallels on this map are narrower than on the Mercator map, the new meridian interval of fifteen degrees allows adequate space for longitude numbers. Caution students again to avoid crowding, perhaps with either vertical or staggered numbers. The best system for most will still be to number alternate meridians, this time by 30s.

At this point in doing these activities, students should be able to work independently to produce neat, accurate maps. As they start Activity M, remind them of this and review these points:

1. Have the needed tools and use them correctly in the ways that have been discussed.
2. Read directions carefully and remember helpful ideas gained from earlier work.
3. Work slowly and check work often to make sure it is as neat and accurate as possible.
4. Use some method, probably numbering alternate meridians, to keep from crowding longitude numbers.
5. Be sure that location dots are clear and that their labels are obvious and readable.
6. Use *estimating*, map *quarters*, and a *straightedge* memory to ensure accurate work.
7. *Lightly* shade maps with colored pencils to distinguish land from water.

Activity   As students become familiar with the various place names used and sometimes repeated in these activities, encourage enrichment work in the form of research into various places and their environs to produce either oral or written reports. Remind students of sources other than encyclopedias as they investigate what these places are. These can include atlases, newspapers, periodicals, television programs, and books.

Visual   Use an overhead transparency of the key to demonstrate to classes the desired map product in this work. Point out the importance of sharp titles and grid line numbers. Emphasize clear dots and legible labels. Use colored transparency markers to demonstrate the value of coloring the land and water. And remind students that maps are useful only if they are neat, accurate, and legible.

Notes:

Activity M: Key

ELLIPTICAL MAP I

Longitude East of Greenwich

Longitude West of Greenwich

0° 10° 20° 30° 40° 50° 60° 70° 80°

180° 150° 120° 90° 60° 30° 0° 30° 60° 90° 120° 150° 180°

BARROW

VLADIVOSTOK

CANTON

PARIS

MONTREAL

CHICAGO

CASABLANCA

PHOENIX

ANTANANARIVO

BRASILIA

BUENOS AIRES

SANTIAGO

TAHITI

WELLINGTON

HOBART

80° 70° 60° 50° 40° 30° 20° 10° 0° 10° 20° 30° 40° 50° 60°

© 1989 J. Weston Walch, Publisher

Where on Earth? Understanding Latitude and Longitude   65T

Activity N: Elliptical Map II

A. Preparing the map   Complete these items on Worksheet N:

1. Title: ELLIPTICAL MAP II
2. Directions: Longitude West of Greenwich, Longitude East of Greenwich
3. Numbers: 0° to 80° , 0° to 70° , 0° to 180°

B. Locating and describing   On the map locate each of the fifteen places below with a dot labeled with that place's name. For each of the ten names below followed by blanks write a good sentence describing that place's relationship to some other thing(s) on earth. Use a world map or atlas for this work.

1. Aral Sea . . 45° N . . 60° E

2. Denver . . 40° N . . 105° W <u>Denver, Colorado's capital, is on the eastern</u> <u>edge of the Rocky</u>_____ .

3. Falkland Islands . . 51° S . . 61° W

4. Lima . . 12° S . . 77° W _____

_____

5. Sri Lanka . . 8° N . . 81° E _____

_____

6. Mexico City . . 19° N . . 99° W

7. New York City . . 41° N . . 74° W _____

_____

8. Port Moresby . . 10° S . . 147° E _____

_____

9. Pretoria . . 26° S . . 28° E _____

_____

10. Reykjavik . . 64° N . . 22° W _____

_____

11. Rio de Janeiro . . 23° S . . 43° W _____

12. Rome . . 42° N . . 13° E _____

13. Sydney . . 34° S . . 151° E _____

_____

14. Tokyo . . 36° N . . 140° E

15. Warsaw . . 52° N . . 21° E _____

_____

Where on Earth? Understanding Latitude and Longitude

Name: _____

Date: _____

Worksheet N: Map

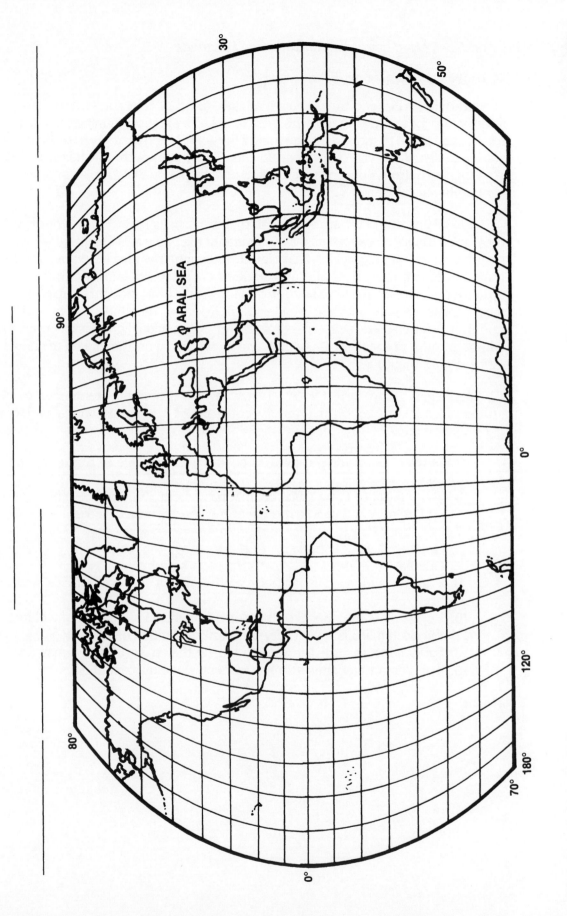

ARAL SEA

30°

50°

90°

0°

80°

120°

180°

70°

0°

0°

Where on Earth? Understanding Latitude and Longitude   67S

Activity N: Notes and Answers

Students will need to use maps, atlases, or other reference materials to get information for writing the ten sentences on relative location. Remind them to try to relate each place to more than one thing if they can. Using a variety of techniques in sentence structure will help them do this. Tell students that in this work good sentence structure, correct punctuation, and proper spelling are as important as geographic accuracy.

Enrichment   Have students read their sentences aloud before the class. As they do so, they can use a wall map to point out the place and the things—nations, rivers, oceans, etc.—to which it is related. To expand the idea of relative location, have students trace the parallel and meridian of each place and name other things that are on or near the same latitude and longitude. Start students thinking about what these places sharing similar latitude and longitude might have in common—time zones, seasons, climate, and length of daylight, for example. This will help them prepare for Lessons 6 and 7, which are on the effects of changing latitude and longitude.

Answers   Plan time for oral review of the descriptive sentences to give students exposure to both properly constructed sentences and a variety of geographic facts.

2. Denver, Colorado's capital, is on the eastern edge of the rocky mountains.
4. The capital of Peru, Lima, is on South America's Pacific coast.
5. Sri Lanka is an island nation near the southern tip of India.
7. New York City is a major harbor on America's east coast.
8. Northeast of Australia is Port Moresby, the capital of Papua New Guinea.
9. Pretoria is located in northern South Africa, a nation at Africa's southern tip.
10. Reykjavik is the capital of the North Atlantic island nation of Iceland.
11. Rio de Janeiro is a large city on Brazil's Atlantic coast.
13. Sydney is in southeastern Australia, on the coast of the Tasman Sea.
15. The Wista River runs through Warsaw, Poland's capital city.

Notes:

Activity N: Key

ELLIPTICAL MAP II

Longitude West of Greenwich

Longitude East of Greenwich

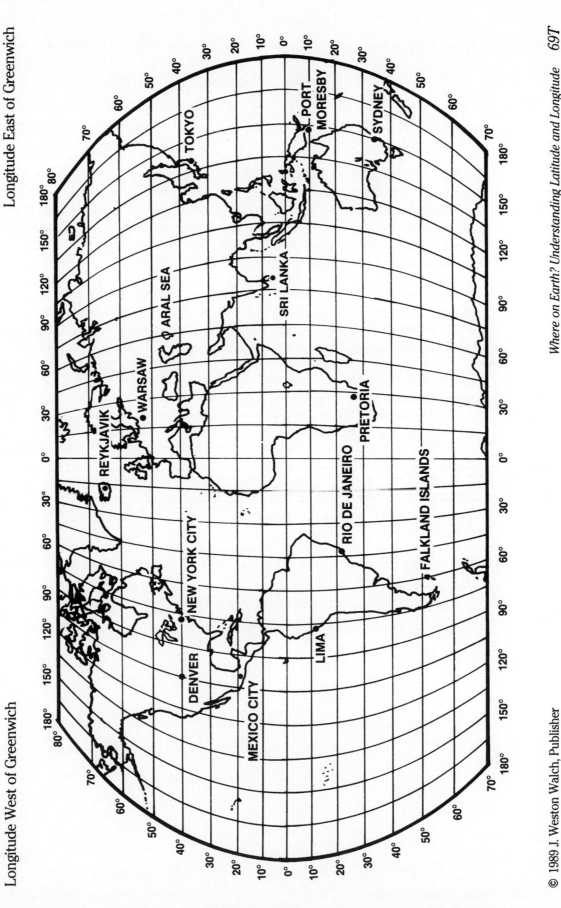

Lesson 6:   Changing Latitude

When people travel either north or south for some distance on the earth's surface, they change their latitude. This change in latitude can produce some interesting effects.

One of the more obvious effects is that a change in latitude usually causes a change in weather patterns. Many factors affect a region's climate, but temperatures are generally colder in areas nearer the poles and warmer in regions closer to the equator. Between these two extremes of climate are regions classified as **temperate**. The milder temperatures here attract large concentrations of population to produce many of the world's large cities.

Because of its effect on climate, latitude has a great influence on how people live. It helps determine the kind of clothes they wear and the type of homes they live in. The plants people grow, the foods they eat, the jobs they have, and the recreation they enjoy are to varying degrees often influenced by latitude.

Upon changing latitude, a careful observer will detect effects of that change. Among these are the location of visible stars at night and the length of shadows seen during the day. The angle of the sun in the sky and, therefore, the warmth of its rays vary greatly with latitude. And latitude affects the length of day and night, particularly in polar regions, where a person may observe the "midnight sun" in midsummer.

Definitions   Use a dictionary to find the meanings of the six words below as they apply to weather and earth locations. Do these activities as directed by your teacher:

(a) On a separate sheet of paper, write a complete, accurate definition of each word.

(b) Use each word correctly in a good sentence.

(c) Be prepared to report orally on the pronunciation, meaning, and use of the words.

1. climate   4. temperate
2. frigid   5. torrid
3. navigation   6. weather (n.)

Lesson 6:   Notes and Answers

"Changing Latitude" may be used for either silent or oral reading. A classroom discussion of its concepts will increase student understanding. Reinforce this discussion with illustrations involving the chalkboard, a world wall map, and the globe. These items can be used to demonstrate different latitudes, climate regions, sun angles, and shadow lengths. Encourage students who have lived or traveled in other latitude areas to discuss observations of daylight hours, star locations, and shadow length that reflect changes from their present latitude. Have students develop a list of local plants, jobs, activities, etc., influenced by the latitude of their community.

Definitions   Inform students which activites are to be done. Remind them to note part-of-speech abbreviations and to keep definitions relevant. Use plenty of oral work in class to ensure that students know the correct meaning and pronunciation of the Definitions words.

1. climate
   - (a) the average weather conditions a region experiences over a prolonged time period
   - (b) They retired to an area with a temperate *climate*.

2. frigid
   - (a) extremely cold
   - (b) Siberia has *frigid* winters.

3. navigation
   - (a) the science of determining the course and location of planes or ships
   - (b) An error in *navigation* caused the plane crash.

4. temperate
   - (a) moderate in terms of climate; neither too hot nor too cold
   - (b) The Mediterranean area has a *temperate* climate.

5. torrid
   - (a) extremely hot
   - (b) The weather in a desert is not always *torrid*.

6. weather (n.)
   - (a) the atmospheric conditions in terms of winds, clouds, temperature, and moisture
   - (b) The poor *weather* delayed the plane's flight.

Notes:

Lesson 7: Changing Longitude

As travel east or west changes one's longitude, some interesting things take place. Some of the effects of changing longitude might be similar to those occurring when latitude is changed, but others may be quite different.

Going to a different longitude can bring about changes in climate, just as a change in latitude might. One may get nearer to or farther from the ocean, into or out of various wind patterns, or closer to or more removed from mountains. These moves, which may be the result of changing either latitude or longitude, can affect the climate.

A unique result of a significant change in longitude is its effect upon time—surely the hour, and maybe even the day. This is because moving east or west pushes a person through different time zones, moving the time ahead or back an hour in each zone. And the traveler who crosses the International Date Line in the Pacific Ocean goes back a whole day when going east or moves ahead a whole day when going west.

These changes can result in "jet lag," a common problem for modern air travelers. One may get worn out from being rushed toward tomorrow when jetting to the east. Another can be slowly dragged through the day when moving with the sun by flying west. Even though their time changes are more gradual, passengers in trains, buses, ships, and cars also have to set their watches periodically to keep in time with their new surroundings.

Definitions Use a dictionary to find the meanings of the six words below as they apply to travel and the earth. Do these activities as directed by your teacher:

(a) On a separate sheet of paper, write a complete, accurate defintion of each word.
(b) Use each word correctly in a good sentence.
(c) Be prepared to report orally on the pronunciation, meaning, and use of the words.

1. axis
2. hemisphere
3. International Date Line
4. lag (n.)
5. sphere
6. time zone

Where on Earth? Understanding Latitude and Longitude

Lesson 7: Notes and Answers

"Changing Longitude" should be read aloud and thoroughly discussed in class. Discuss how live television broadcasts and long-distance phone calls can make people aware of time—even day—changes at different longitudes. Some students may share experiences with "jet lag" on long plane flights.

Factors other than latitude and longitude—winds, mountains, and bodies of water—that influence climate can be reviewed. The need for the International Date Line is another subject that a good, well-illustrated classroom presentation can help students understand.

Definitions Be sure to tell students which activities are to be done. Remind them to note the part-of-speech abbreviation and to keep definitions relevant.

1. axis
   (a) an imaginary straight line through the center of the earth from the North Pole to the South Pole and about which the earth rotates
   (b) The tilt of the earth's *axis* causes the four seasons.

2. hemisphere
   (a) a half of the earth formed by cutting the earth through its center.
   (b) The equator divides the earth into two *hemispheres*.

3. International Date Line
   (a) an imaginary north-south line generally at 180° longitude; the starting point of the new calendar day
   (b) People on the west of the *International Date Line* are a day ahead of those on the east.

4. lag (n.)
   (a) a falling behind; a delay
   (b) The shortage of parts caused a *lag* in production.

5. sphere
   (a) a round, ball-like figure; a ball or globe
   (b) Because it is a *sphere*, a globe can accurately represent the world.

6. time zone
   (a) one of the 24 areas of the world in which the same standard time is used
   (b) Check the television schedule to see when the program is on in your *time zone*.

Notes:

Name: _____ Date: _____ *74S*

Activity O: Additional Places I

Complete worksheet O by filling in the title ADDITIONAL PLACES I, the longitude labels, and the line numbers. Then locate each of the fifteen places below with a dot labeled with that place's name. In each blank below write a good sentence describing that place's relationship to some other thing(s) on earth.

1. Banks Island . . 73° N . . 122° W _____

_____

2. Galapagos Islands . . 0° . . 92° W _____

_____

3. Helsinki . . 61° N . . 25° E _____

_____

4. Lake Superior . . 48° N . . 88° W _____

_____

5. Manila . . 15° N . . 121° E _____

_____

6. Mecca . . 21° N . . 41° E _____

_____

7. Miami . . 26° N . . 81° W _____

_____

8. Murmansk . . 69° N . . 33° E _____

_____

9. Peking . . 40° N . . 116° E _____

_____

10. Quito . . 0° . . 79° W _____

_____

11. Seoul . . 38° N . . 127° E _____

_____

12. Spokane . . 48° N . . 117° W _____

_____

13. Surinam . . 4° N . .57° W _____

_____

14. Timor . . 10° S . .125° E _____

_____

15. Unalaska Island . . 53° N . . 167° W _____

_____

Where on Earth? Understanding Latitude and Longitude

Name: _____

Date: _____

Worksheet O: Map

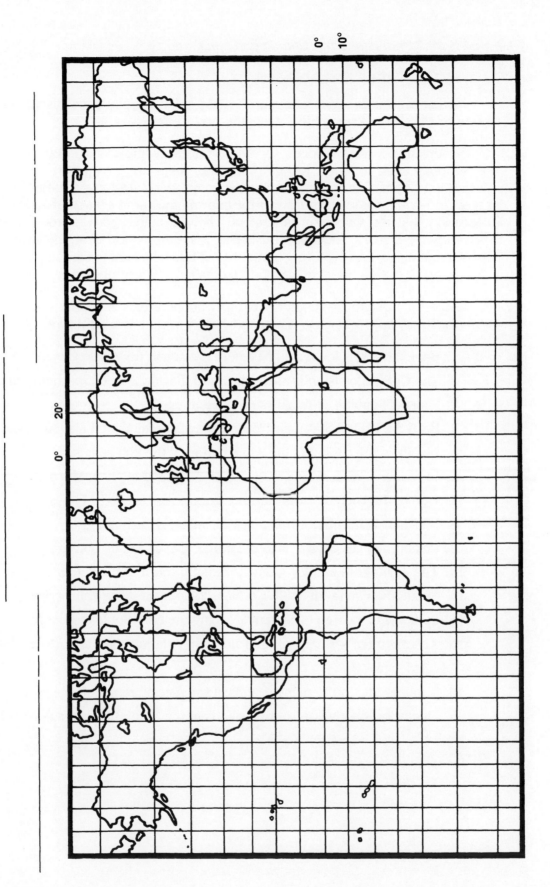

0°
10°

Where on Earth? Understanding Latitude and Longitude   75S

Activity O: Notes and Answers

Worksheet O uses a Mercator map. As it is passed out, use a brief discussion to review this projection's qualities, strengths, and weaknesses.

Be sure students have access to various reference material to gather facts for the sentences on relative location. Remind them to incorporate as much information as possible into sentences that are properly written. As sentences are shared and evaluated in class, discuss the information about a place, in addition to its location, that helps a person understand it better. On the board list items such as size, climate, history, industry, business, trade, transportation, government, tourism, buildings, and culture. Point out how this information can be put into a report ranging from a brief paragraph to a detailed account of several pages.

Answers   Use these sentences to illustrate possible descriptions of relative location. Stress proper English usage and variety in sentence structure.

1. Banks Island is located in Northern Canada in the Arctic Ocean.

2. The Galapagos Islands are in the South Pacific west of South America.

3. Finland's capital, Helsinki, is on the Baltic Sea.

4. Both the United States and Canada have shoreline on Lake Superior.

5. Manila is the capital of the Asian nation of the Philippines.

6. In western Saudi Arabia, near the Red Sea, is the city of Mecca.

7. One of the United States' southernmost cities is Miami, Florida.

8. Murmansk, in the northwest Soviet Union, is near Finland.

9. Peking, China's capital, is in the northeast part of the country.

10. The capital of Ecuador, Quito, is directly south of the Panama Canal.

11. Seoul, the capital of South Korea, is located near the Yellow Sea.

12. Spokane is located in eastern Washington, near the Idaho border.

13. The nation of Surinam is found along the Atlantic coast of northern South America.

14. Timor is one of the many islands in the Asian nation of Indonesia.

15. Unalaska Island is one of the islands at the tip of the Alaska Peninsula.

Notes:

Activity O: Key

ADDITIONAL PLACES I

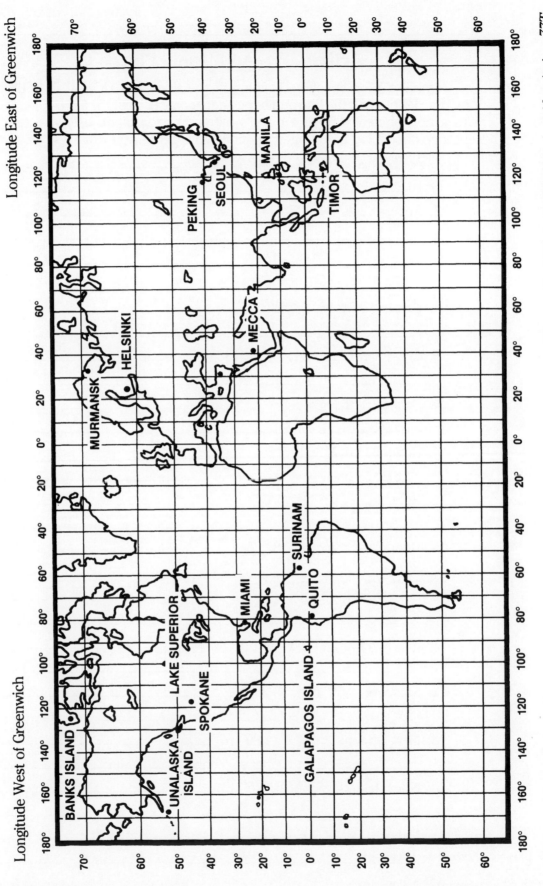

Longitude West of Greenwich

Longitude East of Greenwich

Activity P: Additional Places II

Complete Worksheet P by filling in the title ADDITIONAL PLACES II, the longitude labels, and the line numbers. Then locate each of the fifteen places below with a dot labeled with that place's name. In each blank below write a good sentence describing that place's relationship to some other thing(s) on earth.

1. Anchorage . . 62° N . . 150° W _____

_____

2. Ankara . . 40° N . . 33° E _____

_____

3. Bass Strait . . 40° S . . 146° E _____

_____

4. Dublin . . 53° N . . 6° W _____

_____

5. Great Salt Lake . . 41° N . . 113° W _____

_____

6. Halifax . . 45° N . . 64° W _____

_____

7. Hanoi . . 21° N . . 106° E _____

_____

8. Hokkaido . . 43° N . . 143° E _____

_____

9. Honduras . . 15° N . . 87° W _____

_____

10. Lake Baikal . . 53° N . . 107° E _____

_____

11. Montevideo . . 35° S . . 56° W _____

_____

12. Moscow . . 56° N . . 38° E _____

_____

13. New Orleans . . 30° N . . 90° W _____

_____

14. North Island . . 38° S . . 175° E _____

_____

15. Gabon . . 0° . . 11° E _____

_____

Where on Eartth? Understanding Latitude and Longitude

Name: _____

Date: _____

Worksheet P: Map

10°
0°

30°

0°

Where on Earth? Understanding Latitude and Longitude

Activity P: Notes and Answers

The features, advantages, and disadvantages of the elliptical map on Worksheet P can be discussed when the material is handed out. See that adequate reference material is available for students as they write the sentences on relative location.

Enrichment Have students expand on a relative location sentence by writing a short descriptive paragraph about one of the places. Students should use reference material to add sentences about size, climate, history, industry, business, trade, transportation, government, tourism, buildings, and culture. Use the chalkboard, overhead projector, or handouts to expose the class to examples of good paragraphs. Point out how certain topics can be expanded into more paragraphs for reports and how maps, graphs, and pictures can help illustrate certain points.

Answers Use these sentences as examples of descriptions of relative locations:

1. Anchorage is located at the head of Cook Inlet in southern Alaska.
2. Ankara, the capital of Turkey, is located near the center of that country.
3. Bass Strait separates the island of Tasmania from southeastern Australia.
4. In eastern Ireland, on the coast of the Irish Sea, is the capital city, Dublin.
5. The Great Salt Lake, in northern Utah, is near the borders of Nevada, Idaho, and Wyoming.
6. Halifax, Canada, is on the southern coast of the island of Nova Scotia.
7. The capital of North Vietnam, Hanoi, is located on the Red River.
8. The large, northern island of Japan is Hokkaido.
9. Honduras is a Central American nation with a straight east-west coastline on the Caribbean Sea.
10. Lake Baikal lies in the southeast Soviet Union near Mongolia.
11. Uruguay's capital, Montevideo, is a harbor on the Rio de la Plata.
12. Moscow, located in the western Soviet Union, is the nation's capital city.
13. In southern Louisiana, at the mouth of the Mississippi River, is the city of New Orleans.
14. North Island, the smaller of New Zealand's two main islands, is separated from South Island by Cook Strait.
15. Gabon is a nation located on the west coast of central Africa.

Lesson 7: Changing Longitude

Activity P: Key

ADDITIONAL PLACES II

Longitude West of Greenwich

Longitude East of Greenwich

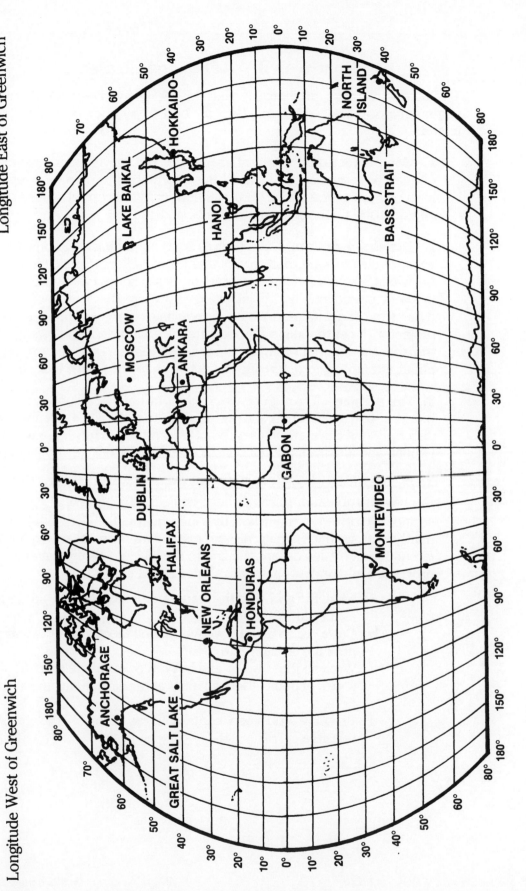

Where on Earth? Understanding Latitude and Longitude   *81T*

Research 3: Additional Projects

Do any of these projects as your teacher may direct for regular class assignments or extra-credit work. Do your best to produce neat, well-organized material.

1. Map projections   Many atlases, texts, and encyclopedias have material on map projections. Use some of this information to prepare a report on at least one projection. Name the projection, include a copy, discuss its qualities, and describe the uses for which it is best suited.

2. The shape of things   Prepare a report consisting of various maps of the *same* bodies of land, but collect them from *different* projections. Maps of Australia, South America, Greenland, or Alaska should work well. Identify the different projections and point out areas where the shapes correspond or differ from map to map. Using a reducing/enlarging copier or overhead projector to get the maps approximately the same size and placing them on transparent material will make comparisons easier. Describe what you learn about attempting to determine the actual shape of a large body of land.

3. The ellipse   Through research find out how an ellipse is made. Use a board, paper, tacks, string, and pen or pencil to make some examples. Attach a description of the method used, pointing out the **periphery**, **axes**, and **foci**. Explain and illustrate the relationship between an ellipse and a cone.

4. Flat map—spherical earth   Use a grid from Activity I or J to illustrate the basic problem in making maps: depicting the spherical earth on a flat surface. Cut the grid, which is $4\frac{1}{2}$ by 9 inches, from the worksheet and place it neatly, with no overlapping, around a standard baseball, which has a 9-inch circumference. Glue or tape the grid to the ball and prepare a report on your procedure and findings. Here are some helpful suggestions:

(a) Wrap the grid, with the equator touching the ball, around the ball as a cylinder.
(b) Cut a series of long, wedge-shaped pieces with the sharp points near the equator of the grid.
(c) Work so that the top and bottom edges of the grid will become a series of points that will meet at the North Pole and at the South Pole.
(d) Preserve and keep continuous as many of the grid lines as possible.

Research 3: Additional Projects *(continued)*

5. Important people   Write a report on one or more of these people, stressing the contributions to surveying and mapmaking:

(a) Clark, William
(b) Fremont, John C.
(c) Lewis, Meriwether

(d) Powell, John W.
(e) Mercator, Gerhardus
(f) Vancouver, George

6. The flat head   Use a marker to draw a head on an inflated heavy balloon or a light plastic beach ball. Make the head complete by putting a face on the front, ears on the sides, and hair on the top and back. Deflate the balloon or ball and, after planning carefully, cut it only enough to get it to lie reasonably flat. Fasten it to a firm surface such as heavy poster board or plywood. Try to get the material into a rectangular shape by stretching it when necessary. Finally, fill in the drawing where there are spaces. Include a report describing the final appearance of the head and the problems related to flattening it.

The project above can also be done by using a simple drawing of the earth and some global grid lines instead of the head. To help form this into a flat world map, make a straight cut from the North Pole to the South Pole between Alaska and the Soviet Union and through the Pacific Ocean. Include a report describing the procedures and results of this project.

7. Changing places   Prepare a chart that compares the average monthly temperatures for cities at different latitudes. Such information, often found in encyclopedias, could be on cities in North Dakota, Nebraska, and Texas. Include a report discussing the differences shown by the chart. Does the information show cooler temperatures at higher latitudes and warmer ones at lower latitudes? Are there any climatic factors other than different latitude that may help explain the temperature differences?

Apply the project above to places at the same latitude, but at different longitudes. Cities in Washington, North Dakota, and Maine could be compared. Report on the climatic factors that might be responsible for temperature differences in places that have the same latitude.

Other projects

Where on Earth? Understanding Latitude and Longitude

Research 3:   Notes

The work in "Additional Projects" will expose students to new ideas and help them develop research and communication skills. Some of the activities may be assigned to the entire class, while others may be selected by students according to individual interests. Add other projects on subjects that have generated questions and discussion.

Reviewing the procedures suggested in the two earlier research sections will help students produce good projects. Research 1:   Notes, page 30T, covered form, library, and materials. Research 2:   Notes, page 40T, presented suggestions for oral reports. Remind classes of good research procedures and effective reporting through either discussions or handouts. Support student project work with library scheduling, reference material, outline maps, and appropriate supplies.

Group research   Working in small groups on certain projects can be a valuable experience for students. They usually can pick up research and reporting skills from one another. There is often value in the teacher's deciding on the composition of the groups because students who will benefit from the experience can be placed together. Also, the assignment of specific projects to the groups can ensure that students will be engaged in appropriate work. Oral presentations are a good culmination for the research efforts of student groups.

Enrichment   Having produced a variety of maps as they have worked on past activities, students should now be interested in techniques that will help them produce clearer, more accurate maps. Present these two ideas for making sharp maps to students when appropriate:

1. Labels   Often grid lines or boundaries restrict the space for names and obscure them if the names are written over these lines. Using correction fluid to cover just enough of the lines to clear a small space for the names will ensure that labels stand out. Students should use this technique with care and only when necessary. Advise them that a pen often writes on the covered area better than a fine-point marker.

2. Color   Good coloring enhances maps but can also obscure labels. One of the best ways to color a map is to shade lightly with colored pencil. An effective variation of this is to shade only a narrow band along borders. This is a particularly useful technique if there are many symbols and labels on the map.

Reading 3:   Preparing for a Test

The information below will help you prepare for a test on the skills and information you have acquired during your work in *Where on Earth?* On the test you will be expected to:

1. Use latitude and longitude to locate places on a world map.
2. Know the meanings of the Definitions words in the Lessons.
3. Understand the information contained in the Lessons and Readings.
4. Write a complete description of either latitude or longitude.

The material you review should include the Activities, Lessons, and Readings from *Where on Earth?* The meanings of the Definitions words should be available, and a world map with clear parallels and meridians will be helpful. Try to use as many of these study techniques as possible:

1. Study with a partner frequently for short periods of time. Give each other places to locate on a world map and quiz one another on word meanings and facts.

2. Review your grids and maps. Pay attention to compass directions and scales. Use estimating, quarters, and a straightedge to locate places accurately.

3. Quiz one another on the meanings of the Definitions words. Be sure your definitions pertain to maps, geography, etc.

4. Read the Lessons and Readings to each other; then explain back what was read. Ask each other questions on the main ideas in these selections. Explain illustrations to each other.

5. Tell one another what latitude or longitude is, how it is measured, and how it affects and helps humans. Write out this same information, read it to each other, and then offer suggestions.

Prepare well for the test by working hard on the suggestions above. Use the test to "show off" what you know. With the right kind of effort, you can do a job that you will be proud of.

Reading 3:   Discussion Notes

When "Preparing for a Test" is handed out, explain to students that many of its study techniques will be useful in studying for tests in all classes. Review this material orally in class. Allowing students to keep the handout will permit them to refer to it as they study.

Be sure that students have the necessary materials to review. If the Activities, Lessons, and Readings have not been kept in folders or notebooks, see that they are available for class use or checkout. Demonstrating the various review techniques orally with classes will be helpful, particularly for those that are not strong in study skills. Do these reviews with classes where appropriate:

1. Use a world wall map to determine the latitude and longitude of several places. Review the cardinal points. Have students use coordinates to locate places on the map. Refresh students on the application of estimating, quarters, and straightedge.

2. Review the meanings of Definitions words. List them on the chalkboard and have students give their definitions. Or, for variety, write definitions on the board and have students match them to the words.

3. Have students read the Lessons and Readings aloud or silently. Then have individuals relate main points to the class in their own words. Use an overhead projector to project diagrams or draw them on the board so students can interpret them to the entire class.

4. Have students suggest words and ideas relevant to latitude or longitude. List these on the chalkboard and have students help number them in a logical order of presentation. Then use these words and ideas in a reasonable sequence of sentences to write a paragraph about latitude or longitude on the board. Do this several times if needed, for many students need help in organizing ideas for summary paragraphs.

Notes:

Name: _____

Date: _____

Test: Map A

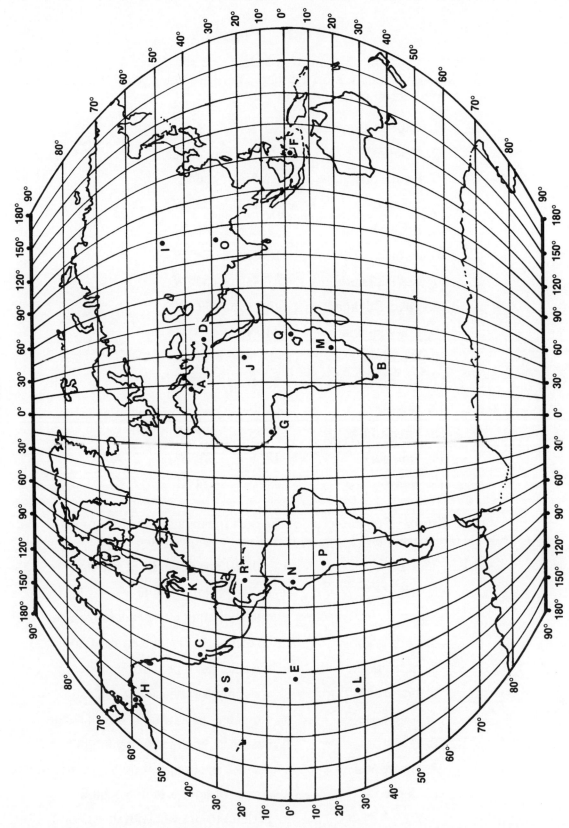

Test: Page 1A

A. Map In front of each item below put the letter from the map that indicates the item's location on the map. There are four extra letters on the map; use all the other letters one time only.

_____	1. Cape of Good Hope	34° S . . .	18° E
_____	2. Celebes	2° S . . .	121° E
_____	3. Damascus	33° N . . .	36° E
_____	4. Detroit	42° N . . .	83° W
_____	5. Ecuador	1° S . . .	79° W
_____	6. Jamaica	18° N . . .	78° W
_____	7. Kodiak Island	57° N . . .	154° W
_____	8. Lake Titicaca	16° S . . .	69° W
_____	9. Los Angeles	34° N . . .	118° W
_____	10. Monrovia	6° N . . .	11° W
_____	11. Mount Everest	28° N . . .	87° E
_____	12. Nairobi	1° S . . .	37° E
_____	13. Pitcairn Island	25° S . . .	133° W
_____	14. Salisbury	18° S . . .	31° E
_____	15. Sicily	38° N . . .	14° E

Definitions Put the letter of the best meaning for each term in the blank. There is one extra answer; use all the others one time only.

_____	1. parallel	a. straight line going from pole to pole
_____	2. minute	b. half of a globe or ball
_____	3. lag	c. one sixtieth of a degree of an angle
_____	4. cartography	d. directly, exactly, in a straight line
_____	5. hemisphere	e. the science of producing maps
_____	6. distortion	f. basic unit for measuring angles
_____	7. longitude	g. a bending or a twisting out of shape
_____	8. due	h. east-west line measuring latitude
_____	9. horizontal	i. distance east or west on the earth's surface
_____	10. degree	j. a lapse of time, a falling behind
		k. parallel to or even with the ground

•   *Where on Earth? Understanding Latitude and Longitude*

Name: _____

Date: _____

Test: Map B

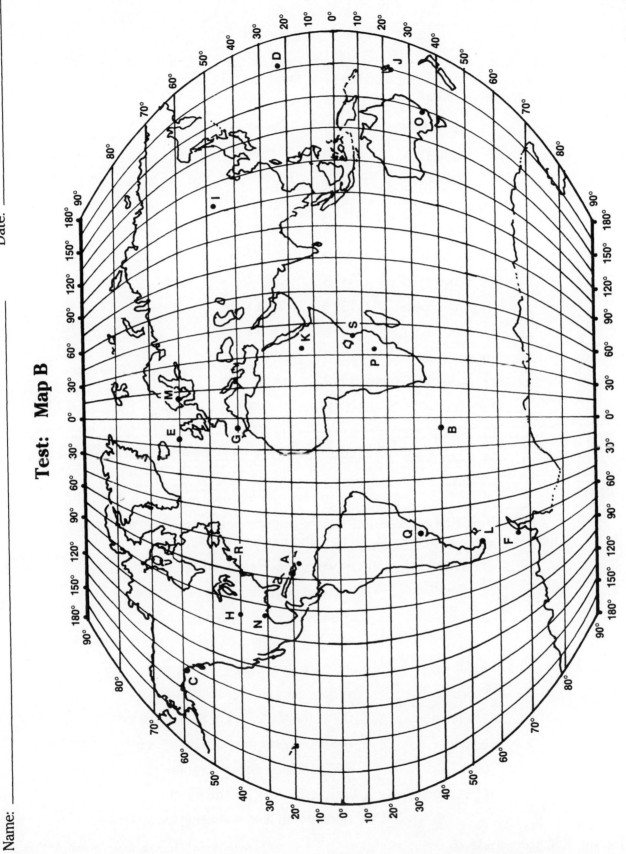

Where on Earth? Understanding Latitude and Longitude   89S

Test: Page 1B

A. Map   In front of each item below put the letter from the map that indicates the item's location on the map. There are four extra letters on the map; use all the other letters one time only.

_____ 1. Adelaide Island   67° S . . . 69° W

_____ 2. Boston   42° N . . . 71° W

_____ 3. Canberra   35° S . . . 149° E

_____ 4. Cape Horn   56° S . . . 67° W

_____ 5. Dar es Salaam   7° S . . . 39° E

_____ 6. Houston   30° N . . . 95° W

_____ 7. Juneau   58° N . . . 135° W

_____ 8. Khartoum   16° N . . . 33° E

_____ 9. Madrid   40° N . . .   4° W

_____ 10. Malawi   13° S . . . 34° E

_____ 11. New Caledonia   22° S . . . 166° E

_____ 12. Oslo   60° N . . . 11° E

_____ 13. Puerto Rico   18° N . . . 67° W

_____ 14. Ulan Bator   48° N . . . 107° E

_____ 15. Uruguay   33° S . . . 57° W

B. Definitions   Put the letter of the best meaning for each term in the blank. There is one extra answer; use all the others one time only.

_____ 1. temperate   a. a pattern of crossing lines

_____ 2. meridian   b. method of placing map on flat surface

_____ 3. projection   c. not having extreme temperatures

_____ 4. pole   d. weather conditions over a period of time

_____ 5. latitude   e. a device to measure distances

_____ 6. vertical   f. a figure with an oval shape

_____ 7. climate   g. the point at the end of the earth's axis

_____ 8. grid   h. distance north or south on the earth's surface

_____ 9. ellipse   i. 1/3600 of a degree of an angle

_____ 10. second   j. upright, running up and down

                          k. north-south line measuring longitude

Where on Earth? Understanding Latitude and Longitude

Test: Page 2

C. True or false Place a **+** in front of the statements that are true and a **0** in front of those that are false.

_____ 1. Latitude does not have to be measured straight north or south from the equator.

_____ 2. The grid lines on all maps run perfectly straight.

_____ 3. There are no longitude measurements at the North Pole.

_____ 4. 60 seconds make a minute; 60 minutes make a degree.

_____ 5. A change of longitude could not affect climate.

_____ 6. The parallels and meridians on a Mercator map are straight lines.

_____ 7. The earth's relation to the sun determines where the prime meridian is located.

_____ 8. As imagined on the earth's surface, meridians are always the same distance apart and never touch.

_____ 9. Changes in latitude normally cause changes in time.

_____ 10. Parallels and meridians can serve as boundary lines.

D. Completion   In the blank before each number write the word that correctly completes the sentence.

_____ 1. The highest value of a longitude reading is _____ (number) degrees.

_____ 2. A _____ angle occurs when a vertical line meets a horizontal.

_____ 3. The _____ Meridian now serves as the world's prime meridian.

_____ 4. The earth measurement that is linked to time change is _____ .

_____ 5. With only a few exceptions, a _____ direction must be given with the latitude or longitude reading.

E. Summary   Write a good paragraph or two on either latitude or longitude. Use the back of this sheet or the next page (back of the map). Title your work with the name of the measurement you are discussing. Be sure to include a good definition that covers the starting point, directions measured, lines used, and the units of measurement. Discuss the effects of changing latitude or longitude, as well as the usefulness of this measurement to humans.

Where on Earth? Understanding Latitude and Longitude

Test: Notes

The test covering the material in *Where on Earth?* has two versions, A and B, of page 1 and its accompanying map. One of the sets of page 1 and its map may be used with classes as an oral review to prepare for the test. Or the two sets may be used to prepare two different forms of the test, A and B, to inhibit copying, to use with different classes, or to give makeup tests.

When the test is reproduced and stapled, be sure the map faces page 1 and the test is stapled in the upper left corner. When the test is opened, the map will be in place for easy reference as page 1 is done. When page 1 is finished, the map can be folded back to become the last page. Student identification is now visible at the top of the test, and the answer for Part E can be written on the back of the map, which is now the last page.

Scoring   If the complete test is to be given one grade, the forty objective items in parts A through D can be given a value of 2 points each for a total of 80, and the summary in Part E can have a value of 20 points. Or, the summary can be given a separate subjective grade, and parts A through D can be scored with a value of $2\frac{1}{2}$ points for each item.

Sample summary   Use this paragraph with classes—either before or after the test, whichever is appropriate to their skills—to illustrate the desired results in summary writing:

Latitude

Latitude is how far north or south a place is on the earth. It is measured from the equator, which is 0° latitude. Latitude measurements must specify north or south to tell which direction they are from the equator. Latitude is measured in degrees because the earth is a sphere. The degrees can be divided into minutes, and then into seconds, for greater accuracy. The highest latitude can go is to 90°, which is at the earth's poles. Different latitudes usually have different climates, warm near the equator and cool near the poles. Latitude is useful to locate places on the earth. Navigators use it and longitude to guide ships or planes, and surveyors use it to establish boundary lines.

Notes:

Test Key: Page 1A

A. Map

1. B	6. R	11. O
2. F	7. H	12. Q
3. D	8. P	13. L
4. K	9. C	14. M
5. N	10. G	15. A

B. Definitions

1. h	6. g
2. c	7. i
3. j	8. d
4. e	9. k
5. b	10. f

Test Key: Page 1B

1. F	9. G
2. R	10. P
3. O	11. J
4. L	12. M
5. S	13. A
6. N	14. I
7. C	15. Q
8. K	

B. Definitions

1. c	6. j
2. k	7. d
3. b	8. a
4. g	9. f
5. h	10. i

Test Key: Page 2

C. True or false

1. 0	6. +
2. 0	7. 0
3. +	8. 0
4. +	9. 0
5. 0	10. +

D. Completion

1. 180
2. right
3. Greenwich
4. longitude
5. compass